SUPERPATRIOTISM

MICHAEL PARENTI

CITY LIGHTS BOOKS
SAN FRANCISCO

Cover design: Stefan Gutermuth
Book design: Nancy J. Peters
Typography: Harvest Graphics

Library of Congress Cataloging-in-Publication Data

Parenti, Michael, 1933-
　　Super patriotism / Michael Parenti.
　　　　p.　cm.
　　Includes bibliographical references and index.
　　ISBN 978-0-87286-433-7
　1. United States—Foreign relations—2001-　2. United States—
Politics and government—2001-　3. Chauvinism and jingoism—
United States.　4. Messianism, Political—United States.
　I. Title.
　　JZ1480.P36 2004
　　323.6'5'0973—dc22　　　　　　　　　　　　　　2004009556

CITY LIGHTS BOOKS are edited by Lawrence Ferlinghetti and
Nancy J. Peters and published at the City Lights Bookstore,
261 Columbus Avenue, San Francisco CA 94133.

www.citylights.com

Additional Books by Michael Parenti

The Assassination of Julius Caesar: A People's History of
Ancient Rome (2003)
To Kill a Nation: The Attack on Yugoslavia (2000)
History as Mystery (1999)
America Besieged (1998)
Blackshirts and Reds (1997)
Dirty Truths (1996)
Against Empire (1995)
Democracy for the Few (7th edition 2001)
Land of Idols: Political Mythology in America (1994)
Inventing Reality: The Politics of News Media (1986,
1993)
Make-Believe Media: The Politics of Entertainment
(1992)
The Sword and the Dollar (1989)
Power and the Powerless (1978)
Ethnic and Political Attitudes (1975)
Trends and Tragedies in American Foreign Policy (1971)
The Anti-Communist Impulse (1969)

ACKNOWLEDGMENTS

Amanda Bellerby, Juliana Baker, Violetta Ettare, and Marisa Tregrossi rendered valuable assistance during the course of writing this book. Jenny Tayloe also gave much appreciated support. My thanks also to Nancy J. Peters and other staff members of City Lights Books for their efforts.

Dedicated to
Robert E. Lane and Helen Lane

TABLE OF CONTENTS

1 WHAT DOES IT MEAN TO LOVE OUR COUNTRY?

AS A GUEST ON RADIO TALK SHOWS, I HAVE criticized aspects of US foreign policy. On one such occasion, an irate listener called to ask me, "Don't you love your country?" Here was someone who saw fit to question my patriotism because I opposed certain policies put forth by US leaders. The caller was manifesting symptoms of what I call *superpatriotism*, the readiness to follow national leaders unquestioningly in their dealings with other countries, especially in confrontations involving military force.

Many people in various countries consider themselves patriotic in that they share common loyalties and national ideals. Generally, in uneventful times, they do not make all that much of such attachments. But during periods of special urgency or national crisis, their leaders take every opportunity to transform their perfunctory patriotism into superpatriotism.

In this country superpatriotism rests on the dubious assumption that the United States is endowed with superior virtue and has a unique history and special place in the world. For the American superpatriot, nationalistic pride, or "Americanism," is placed above every other public consideration. Whether or not superpatriotism is the last refuge of scoundrels, as Dr. Johnson might say, it is a highly emotive force used by political leaders and ordinary citizens to muffle discourse. I think that was what the caller was doing (whether he intended to or not) when asking me if I loved my country. In any case, I would answer his question with another one: What exactly does it mean to love one's country?

☆

Do we love every street and lane, every hill and dale in America? There are so many sights and sites within the USA to which one might grow attached. Yet most of us have had direct exposure to relatively few parts of this nation's vast territory since we lack the time and money to make that meandering trip across its great continental expanse. And what of all the natural beauty in other countries throughout the world? Would I be less a patriot if I am forced to conclude that there are parts of Ireland and

New Zealand that are even more beautiful than the lovely sights of our Pacific Northwest region? Would I be wanting in patriotism if I felt Paris to be more captivating than San Francisco? or the Piazza Navona in Rome more endearing than Rockefeller Center in New York?

Perhaps love of country means loving the American *people*. But even the most gregarious among us know only a tiny portion of the US populace, that vast aggregate of diverse ethnic, religious, and class groups. In any case, any number of superpatriots feel no love at all for certain of their compatriots whose lifestyles, beliefs, ethnicity, or lowly economic status they find repugnant.

It might be that we can love whole peoples in the abstract, feeling a common attachment because we are all Americans. But what actually is so particularly lovable about Americans, even in the abstract? Although many Americans are fine and likable, some are not admirable at all. Among the compatriots who fail to win my affection are ruthless profiteers, corporate swindlers, corrupt and self-serving leaders, bigots, sexists, violent criminals, and rabidly militaristic superpatriots.

☆

Maybe our superpatriots love this country for its history. One would doubt it, since so much of US history is evidently unknown to them: the struggle for free speech that has continued from early colonial times down to this day; the fierce fights for collective bargaining and decent work conditions; the long campaigns to extend the franchise to all citizens including propertyless workers and women; the struggles to abolish slavery, end racial segregation, and extend civil rights, to establish free public education, public health services, environmental and consumer protections, and occupational safety, and to impose a progressive income tax and end wars of aggression, and other such issues of peace and social justice.

Here certainly is a history that can make one feel proud of one's country and love the valiant people who battled for political and economic democracy. But many superpatriots are wretchedly ignorant of this history, especially since so little of it is taught in the schools. How unfortunate, for it would add more substance to their love of country.

Also largely untaught is the darker side of our history. What is there to love about the extermination of Native American Indian nations, a bloodletting that extended over four centuries along with the grabbing of millions of acres of their lands? There is nothing lovable about the systemic kidnapping and enslavement of millions of Africans; the many lynchings and murders of the segregationist era; the latter-day assassinations of Black Panther Party members and other political dissidents; the stealing of half of Mexico (today's Texas, New Mexico, Arizona, California, and a portion of Colorado); the grabbing of Hawaii, Guam, Puerto Rico, and Cuba; the blood-drenched conquest of the Philippines; and the military interventions and wars of aggression against scores of other countries.

Should we love our country for its culture? We Americans can boast of no Shakespeare, Goethe, Cervantes, or Dante, but we still can be proud of our playwrights and poets, our art and opera, our music and dance, our museums and symphony orchestras, our libraries and universities. Yet as far as I can tell, the superpatriots evince relatively little interest in these things. If anything, arts and education are being subjected to merciless budget cuts by those superpatriotic policymakers who prefer to pour our treasure into a gargantuan military budget. They would starve Athens for an ever stronger Sparta.

While we might embrace the good things in our culture, some other aspects are hard to celebrate: the mind abuse of most television and cinematic offerings; the omnipresent, soul-numbing commercialism; the urban and suburban blight and crime-ridden, drug-infested neighborhoods; the proliferation of homeless beggars and shanty encampments; the toxic dumps, strip-mined wastelands, denuded forests, highway vehicular carnage, and widespread contamination of our rivers, bays, and groundwater; the astronomical homicide rates, hate crimes, and child abuse; the widespread emotional depression and spousal abuse; the enormous and still growing gap between the obscenely rich and desperately poor; the overweening rapacity of the giant corporations; the money-driven corruption of much of our public life, and other such dispiriting things.

☆

Some superpatriots claim that they love America because of the freedom it gives us. Yet most of them seem to love freedom only in the abstract, for they cannot stand the dissidence and protests that are the actual practice of a free people. They have trouble tolerating criticisms directed against certain US policies and institutions. If anything, superpatriots show themselves ever ready to support greater political conformity and more repressive measures against heterodoxy.

We might question the quality of the freedom we are said to enjoy, for in truth we are not as free as we often suppose. To be out of step in one's political opinions is often to put one's career in jeopardy—even in a profession like teaching, which professes a dedication to academic freedom.[1] The journalists who work for big media conglomerates and who claim to be untrammeled in their reportage overlook the fact that they are free to say what they like because their bosses like what they say. They rarely, if ever, stray beyond the respectable parameters of the dominant paradigm, and when they do so, it is at their own risk.

The major media in the United States are owned by giant corporations and influenced by rich corporate advertisers who seldom question the doings of the free-market profit system at home and abroad. The assumptions behind US foreign policy go largely unexamined in news analysis and commentary. Those who have critical views regarding corporate power and US global interventionism rarely get an opportunity to reach a mass audience.

☆

Many of our superpatriots love this country because it is considered a land of opportunity, a place where people can succeed if they have the right stuff. But individual success usually comes by prevailing over others. And when it comes to the really big prizes in a competitive, money-driven society, almost all of us are losers or simply noncontestants. Room at the top is limited to a select few, mostly those who have been supremely advantaged in family income and social standing from early in life. Even if the US economy does reward the go-getters who sally forth with exceptional capacity and energy, is the quality of life to be measured by the ability of tireless careerists to excel over others? Even if it were easy to become a multimillionaire in America, what is so great about that? Why should one's ability to make large sums of money be reason to love one's country? What is so admirable about a patriotism based on the cash nexus?

In any case, some Americans have trouble feeling patriotic about the rat race. They do not wish to spend their lives trying to get rich, trying to advantage themselves at the expense of others. They seek to do work that enhances the quality of life for the entire society. If then they are rewarded for their contributions, so much the better, but that is not their prime concern, nor do they feel that the rewards should be so astronomical and nontaxable.

Of course, economic opportunity is not exclusively about getting rich. In America, it is said, millions enjoy the opportunity to "get ahead," to live in comfort and prosperity, short of reaching a stratospheric income. But millions who have worked hard all their lives do not achieve a comfortable life. Upward mobility in the United States is no greater than in other industrial nations. Almost all Americans remain at the same economic level to which they were born. If anything, with the free-market rollback of recent decades, there has been much slippage. It is no longer to be taken for granted that Americans will live better than did their parents. In fact, most are not living as well. Life has become increasingly more stressful and difficult as growing numbers find themselves working harder and harder to stay afloat, with fewer benefits, insufficient income, more stress, and less job security.

Contrary to a popular myth, the USA has the smallest—not the largest—middle-income stratum of the industrial world. Average incomes are rising modestly but only because of more intensive workloads. (In the much-vaunted economic recovery of 2003–2004, investments, sales, and profits climbed, but wages remained flat.) US workers face one of the longest work years in the world. They average only about ten days a year paid vacation, compared to Western European workers who usually get thirty days. Even some Latin American countries mandate one month paid vacation.[2]

America has not been a land of opportunity or economic betterment for the Native American Indians (except for a few casino owners) who have had their lands stolen and their populations sadly reduced by death and disease; nor for industrial workers who still face life-threatening occupational hazards, or who see their jobs being exported to Third World sweatshops; nor for the farm laborers who currently put in long hours at stoop labor for subsistence wages; nor the millions of others who work at joyless dead-end occupations for poverty-level pay, or who manage to attain a higher education only to face a lack of employment opportunities while mired in hopeless debt from student loans.

☆

In sum, it seems that the *America* our superpatriots claim to love is neither a geographical or demographic totality, nor a cultural heritage as such, nor really a land of such unlimited freedom and economic opportunity and prosperity. The superpatriot's *America* is a simplified ideological abstraction, an emotive symbol represented by other abstract symbols like the flag. It is the object of a faithlike devotion, unencumbered by honest history. For the superpatriot, those who do not share in this uncritical Americanism ought to go live in some other country.

1. For further details about the repressive nature of Academia, see my *Dirty Truths* (San Francisco: City Lights, 1996), 235–52.
2. See Doug Henwood, *After the New Economy* (New York: New Press, 2003).

2 "AMERICA—LOVE IT OR LEAVE IT"

DURING THE LATE 1960S, GROWING NUM-
bers of Americans took to the streets to protest the war in
Indochina with its savagely intensive US bombings of
civilian populations in Vietnam, Cambodia, and Laos. In
response, supporters of the war were quick to attack the
demonstrators, both verbally and sometimes even physi-
cally. Steeped in the belief that any war fought by the
United States must ipso facto be a noble undertaking irre-
spective of the human costs, the superpatriots could only
conclude that the antiwar protesters were little better than
traitors who gave aid and comfort to the enemy. In this
instance, our "enemies" were often impoverished Indochinese peasants fighting to liberate their countries from
foreign control.

It was not long before the superpatriotic slogan "America—Love It or Leave It" began appearing on signs and bumper stickers, making its way into the pronouncements of hawkish politicians.

Opponents of the Vietnam War performed many worthy deeds. By galvanizing great numbers of protesters they overthrew the sacrosanct notion that one could not oppose war while the country was actually at war. They contested the widely accepted idea that the United States played a primarily virtuous role in the world. They exposed the selfish material interests behind US overseas interventionism. And many of them began to question the whole elitist political system that produced such policies.

The antiwar movement also publicized the terrible aspects of the Indochina conflict: the villages destroyed and innocent people massacred; the children burned with napalm; the groves, orchards, farms, jungles, wildlife, and peasants themselves poisoned with Agent Orange and other defoliants—information that was largely suppressed by news media and government officials through most of the war.[1] Peace protesters encouraged tax resistance and civil disobedience. They blocked draft boards and induction centers, challenged military recruiters on college campuses, trashed recruitment booths, marched and even rioted in the streets, and generally acted as an insurgent restraint on the war leaders.

The movement reached into the US military itself, creating a climate of dissent that affected the performance of soldiers in Vietnam. During the latter years of the war, infantry squads and platoons sometimes refused to advance deeply into the jungle to make contact with the enemy, some 700 US servicemen deserted, and a few outright mutinies occurred, including at least one of company size. Officers were occasionally the targets of fragmentation grenades from their own men.[2] At home, the peace movement assisted conscientious objectors and other draft resisters, and helped create a climate of opinion against the war.

The dissenters also demonstrated to the world and to the United States itself that there was *another* America, one that did not mindlessly fall into obedient lockstep once the flags were unfurled and the martial music sounded. So while some people cried, "America—love it or leave it," the protesters now responded, "America—change it or lose it."

"America—love it or leave it" is a variation of an older saying that enjoyed currency for more than a century: "My country—right or wrong," a bald proclamation to support the United States government in its conflicts with other governments regardless of the moral issues involved. It is hard to say which posture is more insufferable: the "right-or-wrong" mentality that supports any US action including ones that are arguably wrong, or the "love-it-or-leave-it" mindset that refuses to see anything wrong.

☆

Having witnessed what is done in the name of Americanism, some protesters during the Vietnam era attacked the patriotic symbols of our country. Some burned American flags, thereby convincing more conventional Americans that they were either maniacs or traitors. The war resisters mistakenly put the blame on an entity called *America*, sometimes writing it as "Amerika," intended to give the word a more Germanic Nazi-like tone, or "Amerikkka" with three k's, the initials of the Ku Klux Klan, treating the word itself as a kind of curse. Thus, the protesters mistakenly made America the issue, blaming the nation itself for what was being perpetrated in its name by US leaders.[3]

In so doing, they played directly into the hands of leaders who opportunistically sought to treat their own war policy as a manifestation of true Americanism. America was transformed into an entity that had a living moral existence of its own—supremely virtuous for the flag-wavers, and primarily evil for the flag burners.

"America" was made an issue in another way at about that same time. Many Latin Americans and some Canadians, along with some US peace advocates themselves, were—and still are—opposed to applying the terms "America" and "Americans" to the United States and its citizens. They argue that "America" refers to the entire Western Hemisphere and is not to be appropriated by one particular country in the Americas. In fact, people in other Western Hemispheric countries call themselves Brazilians,

Chileans, Hondurans, Mexicans, Canadians, and so on. They do not identify themselves *nationally* as Americans. They just do not want US citizens to do so.

One might wonder why the appellation "America" should be coveted by anyone at all. It derives from explorer Amerigo Vespucci, who happened to be a despicable slaver and plunderer, every bit as ruthless as Columbus. (In this book I apply the terms "America" and "American" to the United States and its citizens because that is the unavoidable nationalistic idiom I am addressing.)

☆

To this day, US political leaders continue to wrap themselves in the flag, branding all opposition to their policies as attacks against the nation itself. In the 1992 electoral campaign, the older Bush responded to Bill Clinton's criticisms of the economic recession as follows: "My opponent says America is a nation in decline. . . . Well, don't let anyone tell you that America is second-rate, especially someone running for president."[4] Thus, he misrepresented criticisms of his administration's faltering economic policies as an attack on America itself.

This reminds us that *America* would have been made the issue by the superpatriots even if no flags had been burned, and even if nobody had thought to spell it "Amerikkka." "America—love it or leave it" is too inviting a slogan for those who have no desire to subject existing policies to rational scrutiny. By crying "love it or leave it," they can claim a monopoly on patriotism, and denigrate the dissenters for not loving their country.

This continues to be the case. Opponents of US foreign policy are still accused of blaming or hating America. Once again, the protesters are made the issue instead of the policies they are protesting.

In response, we must repeatedly point out that those who criticize the particular policies, leaders, or social conditions of their country do not thereby manifest a deficient loyalty. If the test of patriotism comes only by reflexively falling into lockstep behind the leader whenever the flag is waved, then what we have is a formula for dictatorship, not democracy.

We critics of US policy are not directing our protests against that entity known as America but against particular US leaders who, we feel, do not represent the interests of the American people or any other people, but who advance the goals of a privileged coterie. We are not being anti-American when we criticize the president's policies, no more than we are being "anti-Middletown" and lacking in community spirit if we oppose the policies pursued by the mayor of Middletown, or whatever community. Quite the contrary, our opposition arises out of concern for what is being done to—and in the name of—our country or community.

By the same token we are not being anti-Semitic if we criticize the Israeli government for the incursions and settlements in the occupied territories and for mistreatment of

Palestinians. Some of the most outspoken critics of Israeli policy are themselves Israelis in Israel or Jewish-Americans in the United States who—contrary to the facile psychologistic charge made against them—are not "self-hating Jews." In fact, most happen to be rightly proud of their Jewish heritage. Likewise, we are not showing hatred for Mexico, Italy, Poland, China, or any nation, nationality, or ethnic group if we denounce the particular policies of the Mexican, Italian, Polish, or Chinese governments.

The expression "love it or leave it" means love America *as it is*. Its national institutions and foreign policy are to be treated as above criticism. Those who see some serious problems in US society are deemed unappreciative of the American Way of Life. But the American way is to criticize and debate openly, not to accept unthinkingly the doings of government officials of this or any other country.

☆

The superpatriots tell us that in many countries people do not have the right to criticize their governments. Presumably, we should show gratitude for our freedom to dissent by refraining from dissenting; and if we speak freely and critically, we are proving ourselves ungrateful and therefore unworthy of the right to speak. It seems we "abuse" our rights by simply using them. To repeat, the only thing to match the superpatriots' celebration of our freedom in the abstract is their intolerance toward anyone who actually puts that freedom into practice.

Some superpatriots think that we must not criticize the wonderful country that has given us so much. In fact, we were not *given* anything, certainly not by those who have ruled over our society. The American people, including all the immigrant groups and minorities, have had to fight long and hard for whatever rights they now enjoy. As the son of a poor Italian-American working-class family, I was able to go to school in the first half of the last century only because generations of people before me struggled against the privileged plutocracy for the right of free public education.

So with every other good thing we have been "given." Why should we feel indebted to the ruling moneyed interests for "giving" us the good life, when in fact they furiously resisted every democratic and egalitarian gain that the American people have won over two centuries of struggle, every advance in labor relations, popular electoral participation, public education, environmental and consumer protections, retirement benefits, human services, and other worthwhile measures. Like the good reactionaries they are, the plutocrats continue to oppose most of these things. And in recent decades they have enjoyed increasing success in bringing us back to the old days of Big Money and small democracy.

☆

Getting back to the "love it or leave it" issue, many Americans would be surprised to learn that every year there are substantial numbers of people who permanently leave the United States. Public focus has always been on the waves of immigration to our shores, with little attention given to the outgoing tide. Emigration is a phenomenon that is rarely publicly recognized or even officially recorded—almost as if it were an embarrassment or, worse, a downright un-American phenomenon unworthy of attention.

Despite the deficiencies in data, enough reliable information is available to determine that during much of the twentieth century the United States gained some 30 million newcomers from abroad and lost about 10 million to emigration. Currently more than 150,000 people depart every year. About two-thirds of them are former immigrants who chose to go home or to another country. The remainder are US citizens. Some 300,000 US citizens permanently left the United States in the 1960s, a relatively prosperous decade.[5] And this does not count the others who might have wished to depart but who lacked the wherewithal to do so.

About a third of the US citizens who emigrate each year settle in Canada or Mexico. The next most popular destinations are the United Kingdom and Germany, with Belgium, the Netherlands, Sweden, Norway, and Hong Kong receiving large flows in proportion to their size. Considerable numbers also take up permanent residence in Japan and Australia.[6] Americans emigrate usually for the same reasons that cause people of other nations to leave their homelands: better job opportunities abroad, unhappiness with the quality of life at home, a wish to escape troubled circumstances, attraction to the culture and lifestyle of some other country, a desire to unite with family, and marriage to a foreign national.

In sum, every year tens of thousands of US *citizens* reveal that they are not swept up in any mystique about the unsurpassable greatness of life in America. Since they don't love it, they leave it. Or they may love it but, for whatever reason, they find some other place more promising. Such data contradict the chauvinistic notion that everyone wants to move to America but no one wants to leave.[7]

1. See William Griffith and John Marciano, *Lessons of the Vietnam War* (Totowa, N.J.: Rowman and Allanheld, 1979) for the US media's treatment of the war.

2. Richard Boyle, *Flower of the Dragon: The Breakdown of the U.S. Army in Vietnam* (San Francisco: Ramparts Press, 1972).

3. Such angry spellings are still used in some quarters. Thus an article in *Prison Focus*, no. 18, fall 2003, refers to "the United States of Amerikkka" and "the Amerikkkan social infrastructure."

4. George Bush, acceptance speech, quoted in *New York Times*, 21 August 1992.

5. Jeffrey Passel and Jennifer Peck, "Estimating Emigration from the United States," unpublished paper, 1979 (Population Division, US Bureau of the Census), and studies cited therein.

6. Robert Warren and Ellen Percy Kraly, "The Elusive Exodus: Emigration from the United States," *Population Trends and Public Policy*, no. 8, March 1985.

7. Warren and Kraly, "The Elusive Exodus."

3 THE IMPORTANCE OF BEING "NUMBER ONE"

SUPERPATRIOTS PROUDLY PROCLAIM THAT the United States is "Number One." US presidents are especially afflicted by this *numero uno* syndrome. In the late 1960s President Richard Nixon said: "America is still Number One"(the "still" bespeaking an anxiety about some possible slippage). In the 1988 election campaign, Democratic presidential candidate Michael Dukakis asserted that "we have to make America Number One again." Throughout the 1980s President Ronald Reagan averred that America was both "Number One" and "standing tall—unlike those other nations that slouch or are rather short. In the 1992 campaign, Republican presidential incumbent George Bush reassured us that America is

"Number One" and not "second rate." And years later his son, President George W. Bush, declared that "America is the greatest country in the world," which is just another way of saying we are Number One.

None of these leaders ever explains what is so important about being Number One or the greatest, nor what actually is entailed in occupying the top slot. What specific traits qualify us for that position? What exactly are we Number One *in*? Is it population? No, certainly China walks away with all the awards in that category, followed by India. Geographic size? Russia and Canada have more real estate than does the USA.

Are we Number One in cultural heritage? That might depend on how we define "culture." Taken in the usual sense of arts, crafts, architecture, music, law, mythology, philosophy, literature, and learning, the age-old civilizations of India, Egypt, Iran, Syria, China, Korea, Japan, Greece, Italy, Mexico, Peru, and others too numerous to mention can each lay claim to a cultural heritage that is vastly older and richer than what has developed in North America since the seventeenth-century European settlements. In fact, the European settlers systematically destroyed the resourceful and equitable age-old cultures of the indigenous North American people.

Africa comes down to us as a forbidding "dark continent" of barbarism, but it too is the home of an ancient cultural heritage, rich in art, architecture, music, literature, and mythology. African art has been a source of inspiration and even the object of blatant plagiarism for many famous Western sculptors and painters.[1]

Regarding cultural heritage, consider Iraq. That beleaguered country, attacked and occupied by US forces, is regularly depicted in the US press as in need of our guidance and uplift; we will teach the Iraqis how to govern and care for themselves. Perhaps we should recall that the Iraqis invented writing, founded the first school of astronomy, and developed modern mathematics, using a kind of Pythagorean theorem 1,700 years before Pythagoras. Beginning around A.D. 800, they founded universities that imported teachers from throughout the civilized world to teach medicine, mathematics, philosophy, theology, literature, and poetry (at a time when Christian Europe had long suppressed serious study of such subjects). For thousands of years, the Iraqis wrote some of the greatest poetry, history, and sagas in the world, and fashioned some of the most imposing stone, metal, and clay artworks. With the Code of Hammurabi, they brought forth the first legal system that protected the weak, the widowed, and the orphaned. Twelve thousand years ago, they invented irrigated farming, and became so proficient at it that in the 1990s, despite sanctions imposed by the West, they still managed to produce all the food they needed.[2]

And in the present century, though depicted in the US press as tribal and backward and in need of our enlightened guidance, the Iraqis continued to be a highly capable and well-trained people with noted achievements in science, engineering, literature, and the arts—not to mention their resourcefulness in waging an armed resistance against powerful US occupation forces.

☆

Culture aside, is America Number One in finance? The major banks in the world are now Japanese, I am told. And some American top financiers are too busy plundering pension funds and small investors to set any admirable world standards in banking.

We used to be Number One in steel production and other heavy industries. But our superpatriotic corporate leaders have taken to exporting US industries to cheaper overseas labor markets so they can rake in higher profits.

Is the United States tops in trade? We Americans are supposed to be the world's best salesmen, but in fact most of the world seems to be outselling us, as is evident from the immense trade deficits that the USA runs up annually. Anyone who has bought durable-use consumer goods in recent years cannot help noticing how many of them seem to be made in the sweatshops of China, Indonesia, Taiwan, or some other Third World nation.

Perhaps this country is Number One in cuisine? Certainly the USA has produced some fine cooking schools and chefs, along with a variety of natural food delights and other gastronomic innovations. But then one thinks of China, France, India, Italy, Greece, Ethiopia, Japan, and any number of other nations whose national cuisines are cause for salivating. In sheer market penetration, however, the United States, with its McDonald's and other fast-food chains burgeoning overseas, is unsurpassed in corrupting the tastebuds of millions of people around the world. But that really is nothing to be proud of. And when the superpatriots talk about being Number One, I think they have something more momentous in mind than nouvelle cuisine or greasy, salty, chemical-ridden, genetically engineered hamburgers.

What then is the United States Number One in? As best I can tell, it comes down to two things: wealth and military might. Let us consider these in turn. Wealth does not reside in a society as an undifferentiated aggregate. It is possessed by particular individuals and their corporate organizations and financial institutions. In the United States the vast majority of us are not rich. A tiny fraction of one percent own a lion's share of the wealth. There is a modestly sized middle class that manages to do well enough but knows no certain economic security. Then there is a large lower-middle to low-income population, some 80 percent of our population, who live with chronic money concerns and little or no net financial assets. And below them, are millions of extremely poor who endure severe deprivation at the very bottom of the pile.[3]

As noted in chapter one, there are Western European social democracies that have a more equitable standard of living and superior benefits and public services than are found in the United States. In that sense, they are, if not richer than we, certainly freer from poverty and want. To celebrate our national wealth, then, one might first consider how it is distributed and used. To talk about *our* wealth is like talking about *our* oil in Texas or the Middle East. We the people do not own US oil reserves at home and abroad. The world's oil supply is controlled by a few giant cartels, owned by a relatively small number of obscenely rich individuals. As with oil, so with *our* wealth in general: a select coterie at the very top of the economic ladder control more of it than all the rest of us combined. We just produce it with our hard work. They pocket it.

☆

Wealth aside, consider the other thing that the United States is Number One in: military might. We need to question why being Number One in kill capacity is such a great accomplishment. In 1992, the first President Bush said, "We must be a military superpower."[4] The celebration of military prowess as a sign of national greatness is predicated on the questionable assumption that such power is for laudatory purposes only.

President Reagan once exclaimed, "We love America because America is the greatest." This view implies that if America were not so great (read strong), we would not find it so lovable. Our love seems predicated on the country's being bigger and more powerful than other nations. What then of peoples who inhabit these lesser lands that cannot claim such "greatness"? For instance, can citizens of

Luxembourg love their country? Luxembourg can never aspire to be Number One. In fact, it must be about Number 138, not that far ahead of Liechtenstein in the greatness of its military might. Do people from Luxembourg walk about shamefaced because they rank so low? Do they try to pass themselves off as French or German? When asked if they love their country, do they mumble: "What is there to love? A few border police, no navy, no real air force."

While political leaders boast about US military strength, they say nothing about its *costs*: the distorted technology, material waste, ecological devastation, enormous debt and high taxes, and the neglect of social needs and infrastructure—not to mention the terrible consequences that other countries must endure when finding themselves on the receiving end of this superpower's military might.

☆

The United States is Number One in certain other things that are rarely if ever mentioned by our leaders. Compared to other industrial nations, we are Number One in homicides and death by firearms. The US murder rate among young males is twenty times higher than in Western Europe and forty times that of Japan.[5] We are Number One in per capita prison population and in financial bailouts, trade imbalances, and budget deficits.

This wealthiest of all nations has a public debt that is the largest in the world. We also have schools that are falling apart, public hospitals that are closing down, and all sorts of essential public services that are being cut back for lack of funds. So alongside the highly concentrated private wealth there exists a growing public poverty. We are tops among the Western industrial nations in the number of preschoolers living in poverty and the number of people lacking medical insurance. The USA is also Number One in family farms that are going broke, genetically modified foods, the factory-farm use of pesticides and herbicides, and the amounts of antibiotics and hormones injected into livestock.

The United States is Number One in managers per employees. A country like Japan, supposedly encumbered with traditional hierarchy, has less than one-third the number of managers per employees.[6] In other words, while the leaders of US industry complain about bloated government bureaucracies, they themselves populate top-heavy bloated corporate bureaucracies.

The USA is also Number One among industrial nations in income inequality and executive salaries. The number of multimillionaires has increased by over 80 percent in the last two decades. We also have the largest number of newly minted billionaires. Average remuneration for chief executive officers (CEOs) of corporations is anywhere from two to six times higher than CEOs abroad. A *Fortune* magazine survey of a hundred of the nation's largest corporations found that the typical CEO enjoyed a 14 percent rise in income in 2002, bringing his or her total yearly pay to an average of more than $13 million, irrespective of whatever scandals or slumps the company underwent. Meanwhile, stock options for these top tycoons continued to expand, in some instances to astronomical levels. Thus the former chairman of Tenet Healthcare, the nation's second largest hospital chain, pulled in stock options worth $111 million in 2002.[7] At the same time, in many of these companies, employees were laid off or endured wage freezes, cutbacks in benefits, or disappearing pension funds.

In sum, before bragging in the abstract about how America is the greatest, the superpatriots ought to attend to the unsettling specifics. Number One indeed, but at what price?

1. Eduardo Galeano, *Upside Down* (New York: Henry Holt, 2000), 55–56, 72–73.
2. For more on Iraqi History, see http://lexicorient.com/cgi-bin/eo-direct-frame.pl. http://i-cias.com/e.o/iraq_5.htm.
3. Stephen Rose, *The American Profile Poster: Who Owns What* (New York: Pantheon, 1986); and my "The Very Rich Are Out of Sight" <www.michaelparenti.org>.
4. Acceptance speech before the Republican national convention, *New York Times*, 21 August 1992.
5. World Health Organization Statistics cited in *New York Times*, 27 June 1990; also James Patterson and Peter Kim, *The Day America Told the Truth* (New York: Penguin, 1992), 131.
6. *Yearbook of Labor Statistics 1989–90* (Geneva: International Labor Organization, 1990), 120–186; *OECD Economic Outlook* (Paris:

Organization for Economic Cooperation and Development, 1991), 136.

7. The *Fortune* survey and stock option information is reported in John Cassidy, "Business as Usual," *New Yorker*, 4 August 2003.

4 MILITARY PATRIOTISM: FOR FLAG AND MISSILE

A KEY COMPONENT OF SUPERPATRIOTISM is its uncritical dedication to military glory and nation-state aggrandizement. Patriotic ceremonies are more likely to commemorate the nation's *military* history than its history of struggle for politico-economic equality, peace, and social justice. Consider the many monuments, memorials, parades, public gatherings, movies, and television documentaries that evoke images of war: Valley Forge, the Alamo, Gettysburg, the Winning of the West (that is, the extermination of Native American nations), D-Day, the flag-raising on Iwo Jima, and the like. Our country right or wrong, but mostly our country at war or ready for war.

July 4th Independence Day celebrations and other

national holidays such as Veteran's Day (November 11th) in cities and towns across the nation would be incomplete without the martial music and parading veterans. July 4th fireworks are a benign replication of "the rocket's red glare, the bombs bursting in air," as goes our top patriotic song. Not many years ago, television stations would sign off the air at night by playing the national anthem, accompanied by footage of aircraft carriers slicing through the seas, fighter jets cutting across the sky, and other militaristic images. Some stations still do.

Young men and women join the US armed forces out of a desire to serve their country—we are told. But critics note that the lack of employment opportunities in civilian life is often the real spur to recruitment; it is called *economic conscription*. The promise of career training, travel, and scholarships, or just the simple guarantee of regular meals and pay, are a paramount part of the lure. And if one is an officer, the pay, pension, and lifestyle are quite good indeed. Military recruiters themselves say little about patriotic sacrifice—such as dying for your country or getting your limbs blown off or your eyesight or brain destroyed in combat. Instead, recruitment appeals focus on career opportunities and personal fulfillment: "Be all you can be" says one Army recruitment poster. "Expand your experience," says a Navy television advertisement.

Still, the military is seen as the special repository of national devotion and patriotic sacrifice. Even some of the military's weapons systems are endowed with nationalistic and patriotic sounding names. There were the "Liberty Ships" of World War II, and more recently the "Minuteman Missile," the "Frontier Missile," the "Patriot Missile," and navel vessels such as the *USS Constitution*, the *USS Liberty*, and the *USS Abraham Lincoln*. And if that is not enough, the second US war against Iraq was accorded the code name "Operation Enduring Freedom"—without the slightest trace of intended irony.

The message is clear: patriotism and militarism go together. A flag in one hand, a weapon in the other, that is what makes America great; that is what supposedly makes us free and independent, safe and prosperous.

☆

The marriage of militarism to patriotism makes it difficult to criticize the enormously bloated military budgets yearly allocated by the US Congress, reaching well beyond $500 billion by 2003 (including the sums spent on the war in Iraq). According to a General Accounting Office investigation, the Pentagon somehow lost track of the enormous sum of $1.1 trillion over the last several decades! As noted in one newspaper, "waste has become ingrained in the Defense budget because opposition to defense spending is portrayed as unpatriotic."[1] Imagine if the Department of Housing and Human Services or the Social Security administration had "misplaced" such a titanic sum; many members of Congress would ring the welkin with demands for drastic cutbacks and punitive reform.

One would think that tolerating massive thievery in the Pentagon is itself a rather unpatriotic thing. As Representative Henry Waxman (D-Calif.) charged, the Pentagon has failed to address financial problems that dwarf those of anyone else. "While vast sums of money are being siphoned off into hidden coffers, America's schools, hospitals and public services are facing cutbacks and closures." If those missing billions were returned to the states and cities on a pro-rata basis, argued Waxman, the fiscal crises that state and local governments were suffering would have been solved, and life in America would be better for many of us.[2]

With the link between militarism and patriotism so firmly fixed, any criticism of the military runs the risk of being condemned as unpatriotic. The film company Mirimax endured endless headaches trying to decide when to release its darkly satirical movie, *Buffalo Soldiers*, about bored, thieving, drug-dealing US soldiers stationed in Germany. The film was attacked by conservative groups as "flamboyantly unpatriotic fare" and "demoralizing" to our troops "who have put their lives on the line defending America and its freedoms." Thus, critical issues about the mistreatment of enemy prisoners and killing of unarmed civilians, massive budgetary corruption and Pentagon mismanagement, and drug problems in the ranks are ignored or downplayed.[3]

☆

Militaristic superpatriotism is closely linked to the macho values of violent dominance. In the aftermath of the US Civil War, a chaplain for the Grand Army of the Republic, a veterans' group, conflated militaristic patriotism and manliness with these words, "The Union stands for American Manhood, a manhood strong in physical courage. . . . being once aroused [it] has the spirit of that order given by Gen. Dix: 'If any man dare insult the American flag, shoot him on the spot.'"[4] The Italian fascist leader, Benito Mussolini, summed it up when he said a man must be "a husband, a father and a soldier." In other words, a "real man" must fulfill the patriarchal and patriotic roles as one, ruling over his family as a tyrant while serving the tyrant who rules over his country. In one phrase Mussolini makes clear that patriarchy and militarism are essential components of reactionary patriotism. *Il Duce* himself was almost a caricature of the macho leader, strutting about in jackboots and a uniform laden with medals, with chin jutting out in a puffed-up tough-guy posture. The superpatriot is a militarist, and the militarist in turn is a swaggering he-man patriarch, celebrating the male chauvinist values of force and power.

One US Air Force captain, reminiscing about his bombing attacks against the peasant population of Vietnam, made an explicit connection between high-tech war, machismo, mindless patriotism, and nation-state moral supremacy: "Flying a fighter plane is . . . a macho thing, maybe—an extension of your manhood. You do it, concentrate on it, and under the circumstances it was damn hard for me to get worried about the political implications of the war. It was a chance for us to show our military power. We're basically patriotic, conservative people. And we're blameless."[5]

The women who now enter the armed forces make the grade only if they are a close approximation of the male model in toughness and force. That women recruits would inject a kinder, gentler, more humane modus operandi into the ranks is an idea that has never been seriously entertained by the military brass or anyone else, as far as I know.

☆

War is often a great incitement to state idolatry, especially when people think they are going to win easily. Reflecting on the war fever she observed in Paris on the eve of the Franco-Prussian war of 1870, an American woman wrote: "The war, the war, there is no other topic. Utter strangers would stop to discuss the situation. The confidence in the generals and the army was immense. It was to be one long but straight march to Berlin; not a soul doubted it." Thousands crowded the Place de la Concorde nightly, indulging in frenzied dancing. Boulevard windows were thick with flags. And anyone who dared question the wisdom of the war was jeered as a "Prussian spy" and chased down the street.[6] But the chauvinist ardor cooled precipitously when the war brought a disastrous defeat for France.

Something similar happened in the United States with the onset of the Civil War in 1861. There was an eruption of patriotic sentiment in the North coupled with the anticipation of an early victory over the Southern secessionists. But after a year of conflict, during which the Union Army suffered a number of military disasters, patriotic fervor plummeted. Lincoln's efforts to rally the populace for a long and costly conflict met with little enthusiasm.[7] Only after Union forces finally emerged victorious in 1865 did patriotic sentiment regain its momentum.

Like all bullies, superpatriots are at their best when picking on someone smaller and weaker. They like "wars" that are hardly worthy of the name, steeply one-sided assaults that bring quick and easy victory with few American casualties. In 2003, on the eve of the US invasion of Iraq, a lieutenant colonel in the US Marines told his troops, "We are going to slaughter the 51st Mechanized Division," an Iraqi unit. It would not be a fair fight, he said. "My idea of a fair fight is clubbing baby harp seals. We will hit them with everything we have."[8] Enjoying a total advantage in firepower and airpower, he gleefully glorified a military engagement that was hardly more than a one-sided slaughter.

The late comedian Bill Hicks once remarked that the people who dismayed him the most at the end of the first Gulf War (a quick easy victory) were the ones who said, "Well, the war made us feel better about ourselves." "Who are these people with such low self-esteem," Hicks asked, "that they need a war to feel better about themselves? I saw them on the news, waving their flags. Could I recommend instead of war to make you feel better about yourself, perhaps sit-ups? Maybe a fruit cup? A walk around the block at dusk?"[9]

Many superpatriots were exhilarated by the US aggressions perpetrated against Grenada, Panama, and Iraq. Ronald Reagan, the Conqueror of Grenada (a tiny island nation of 102,000 inhabitants), reflecting upon his great military victory, hailed the venture as an example of how the USA brings democracy and prosperity to other lands. In fact, after Grenada was "liberated" by Reagan, its unemployment rate skyrocketed. The new enterprises and development projects and health and educational programs initiated by the revolutionary New Jewel movement were wiped out. Public services were privatized or abolished outright. Farm collectives were driven off the land to make way for privately owned golf courses to accommodate North American tourists. Grenada was again made safe for neoliberal capital penetration.[10] The Reagan invasion served notice to the Caribbean nations that they had better not try to develop a collectivist social order that goes against the corporate free-market way of doing things.

The same story can be told about Panama. The 1989 US invasion brought a sharp increase in unemployment, homelessness, economic misery, crime, drugs, and government corruption.[11] Nothing was gained except the deaths of several thousand Panamanians, a US occupation, political repression of reformist groups, and a boost in the opinion polls for President George H. W. Bush. So with Iraq, which once had the best standard of living in the Middle East. The 1991 attack on the country and the subsequent dozen years of sanctions left that country with a shattered technological infrastructure, a destroyed agriculture base, cholera and typhoid epidemics, a spectacular rise in cancer rates in the areas contaminated with depleted uranium, and over 200,000 deaths.[12] So too with the younger Bush's invasions of Afghanistan in 2002 and Iraq in 2003, bringing more death, destruction, and deeper poverty for the people of those countries, and a sharp—if temporary—hike in popularity for his presidency.

☆

For all their militarism, American superpatriots dislike difficult, costly wars, such as the one in Vietnam. Here was a small country but one still strong enough to inflict heavy casualties on US forces while enduring a terrible pounding itself. The superpatriots complained that we fought in Vietnam "with one hand tied behind our backs," exercising too much restraint—despite the fact that the United States dropped more explosives on Indochina than fell in all of World War II, leaving several million Indochinese dead, and millions more maimed or missing. The jingoists would have applauded the use of nuclear weapons in Vietnam. That certainly would have finished off all those troublesome Communist rebels, and US forces would have "won" the war, creating another radioactive cemetery and calling it peace.

The second war in Iraq is another case. The swift and apparently decisive victory in the spring of 2003 evoked much enthusiasm from the patriotic hawks. But in the months that followed, US occupation forces found themselves unexpectedly embroiled in a people's resistance, enduring more than thirty daily guerrilla attacks that inflicted mounting US casualties. Suddenly facing a protracted and costly struggle, the US public no longer registered such a gung-ho approval rating for the president or for the military venture in Iraq. War is much less fun when the other side starts hitting back with any deadly efficacy.

1. "Military Waste Under Fire," *San Francisco Chronicle*, 18 May 2003.

2. See Waxman's quotation and other comments in Gar Smith, letter to *San Francisco Chronicle*, 18 August 2003.

3. See comments by Patricia Pearson, "Is the Military Above Negative Portrayals?" *USA Today*, 6 August 2003.

4. Cecilia Elizabeth O'Leary, *To Die For: The Paradox of American Patriotism* (Princeton, N.J.: Princeton University Press, 1999), 55.

5. Quoted in John Vinocur, "Pilots Who Hit Hanoi Meet to Remember—and Forget," *New York Times*, 14 April 1978.

6. Quoted in Ralph Martin, *Jennie, The Life of Lady Randolph Churchill 1854–1895* (New York: New American Library, 1970), 37.

7. O'Leary, *To Die For*, 27–28.

8. Lt. Col. Bryan McCoy, quoted in *San Francisco Chronicle*, 10 November 2003.

9. Hicks, quoted in Nick Zaino, "Can You Believe This?" *Progressive*, February 2003.

10. Daniel Lazare, "Reagan's Seven Big Lies about Grenada," *In These Times*, November 16, 1983; "A Tottering Structure of Lies," *Sojourner*, December 1983; and Michael Massing, "Grenada Before and After," *Atlantic Monthly*, February 1984.

11. Clarence Lusane, "Aftermath of the U.S. Invasion: Racism and Resistance in Panama," *CovertAction Information Bulletin*, Spring 1991.

12. United Nations, *The Impact of War on Iraq*, Report to the Secretary-General on Humanitarian Needs in Iraq in the Immediate Post-Crisis Environment by a Mission to the Area Led by Mr. Martti Ahsaari, Under-Secretary-General for Administration and Management, 20 March 1991.

5 "USA! USA!"
SPORTS FOR SUPERPATRIOTS

SUPERPATRIOTISM EXTENDS INTO THE world of sports. At every major league baseball game, just before play begins, a voice comes over the loud speaker telling everyone to rise to their feet and remove their hats. The stadium's giant electronic screen projects an image of the American flag flapping vigorously in the wind. A vocalist belts out "The Star Spangled Banner." Many spectators sing along, while the players of each team stand in lines, reverently holding their caps to their chests.

In the previous chapter, we noted how militarism is linked to patriotism. And as the above example suggests, so is sports. Thus it is a short step to weaving all three together—as when militaristic patriotic hype is injected into major sporting events. During the Gulf War of 1991, the televised National Football League conference championship began with US Army, Navy, Marine, and Air Force personnel in parade dress, carrying flags down the field as the crowd chanted "USA! USA!" That same year's Superbowl game, on ABC-TV, featured gigantic patriotic floats and fans waving a sea of little American flags while singing patriotic songs. A taped appearance by the first President Bush and his wife Barbara was flashed across the screen. At half-time, ABC news anchorman Peter Jennings came on with an upbeat update on the US destruction of Iraq.

During that same Gulf War just about every basketball team in the National Basketball Association, and some college teams too, had American-flag patches sewn onto their uniforms (in imitation of the ones on US combat uniforms). As one announcer pointed out, it was "in support of our efforts in the Gulf." Flag patches became a permanent fixture for the uniforms of many basketball, football, and baseball teams at the professional, college, and high school levels.

In a joint venture with the Department of Defense, the National Football League sponsored a sixty-minute documentary on Operation Desert Storm (the official name of the 1991 attack on Iraq). Steve Sobol, president of NFL Films, proudly maintained: "I don't want to say that war is the same as football. But . . . the same spirit and ideology that football glorifies is also the spirit necessary for a successful military endeavor."

In the aftermath of the terrorist attacks on the World Trade Center and the Pentagon in September 2001, and again during the US invasion of Iraq in 2003, sporting events took on an increasingly patriotic hue, especially in their televised presentations. Impressions of the American flag along with glowing images of "our fighting men and women" floated across the TV screen in pregame warm-ups and during breaks in the play. Some of the game-time commercials even featured US military personnel using the advertised products.

Along with militarism and patriotism, sporting events sometimes enlist another nationalistic adjunct: religion. Some football players, moved by a divine urge—or perhaps by a desire to maximize their time on camera—assume a posture of prayer in the end zone after scoring a touchdown. Some genuflect and make the sign of the cross. During key moments of play other team members on the benches will affect a praying posture, an act of devotion that is often rewarded with camera attention. Some baseball hitters are given to tapping different parts of their head and upper body in what seems like a religious ritual, or maybe it's just some voodoo thing. One famous baseball slugger, Barry Bonds, upon hitting a home run, points with both his hands up to the sky as he begins his trot around the bases, thereby claiming divine assistance for his feat. God, it seems, is a San Francisco Giant fan. (In fact, an investigation in early 2004 implicating Bond in the use of performance-enhancement drugs suggests that his inspiration may be less ethereal and more substantive.)

☆

When it comes to *international* sporting events, the "Number One" syndrome is activated full force. Instead of bringing Americans closer to other nations, international contests seem to fuel a winning-is-everything mentality, an unrestrained aggressive rah-rah competitiveness that defeats the purpose of goodwill games.

During the Cold War, for instance, contests between the United States and the Soviet Union always provided occasion for furious flag-waving and Red-bashing. In the Reagan era, when Soviet-hating was at its height, the US Olympic hockey team defeated a second-string Soviet team at Lake Placid, New York. The screaming crowd could hardly contain itself. The ABC *Nightline* announcer crowed: "The Americans withstood an all-out Soviet assault." In an after-game interview, the US hockey coach said that he had reassured his players they "have something the Russians don't have . . . the American belief that we can succeed at anything we do." Had the Soviets claimed such a faith in their own invincibility, it would have been taken as evidence of their aggrandizing ways.

When asked how was it that his team did so well, this same coach said that some time earlier he had traveled to the Soviet Union and had met with Soviet hockey coaches, who had shown him the new fast-breaking techniques they had developed. He then put these methods to good use with his own team. No comment was proffered by him or the interviewer regarding the generosity shown by the Soviet coaches in sharing their skills with the American visitor, whom they seemed to treat more as a fellow sportsman than an arch–Cold War rival.

When the Soviet Union beat the USA in basketball in the 1988 Olympics, NBC treated it as the end of civilization as we know it. In postgame commentaries, NBC announcers described the US team as seriously handicapped by insufficient practice time and the loss of a key player and thus unable to withstand "the Soviet onslaught." The Soviets, it seems, "never let up their attack," and were a "relentless juggernaut." The impression left was that the American players were facing the Red Army rather than another basketball team. After this defeat the United States decided to enter professional basketball players in the Olympics, making sure there would be no more basketball defeats at the hands of the Communists or anyone else.

Four years later in the 1992 Olympics, American fans were able to roar their delight when seven-foot NBA pros pulverized a ragged team from Zaire, composed of kids who had to work for a living, who barely raised enough money to get to the Games, and who had begun to practice in their spare time only a few months before. Many Americans love the advantage of a highly tilted playing field. So intense is their need to see America win that they are not too particular about the quality of the victory and the fairness of the contest. For them, America always gets its way! America is the greatest! Don't mess with America!

The Olympics are supposed to promote international good will and sportsmanship, an appreciation of athletes from all nations, not a shrill nationalism. But at the 1996 Olympic Games hosted in Atlanta, Ga., American spectators seldom if ever applauded the foreign teams or showed any sign of hospitality toward them. And they practically hissed with rage when the Cuban women's volleyball team beat the US team.

It is quite natural for US viewers to favor their own country in international athletic contests, but it is something else to shout with such unrestrained partisan intensity when the Americans win, or lapse into sullen silence or hisses when they lose, begrudging even a display of polite applause for the other team. So we are treated to the spectacle of our compatriots frantically waving hundreds of little American flags, loudly chanting "USA! USA!" and drowning out the applause or cheers that other spectators might express for athletes of other nationalities.

☆

Such ungracious partisanship is encouraged by the television coverage itself, which has been marked by an undisguised US chauvinism. ABC's presentation of the 1984 Summer Olympics so shamelessly favored the performances of US athletes as to evoke an official reprimand from the normally placid International Olympic Committee. Similar complaints were registered by South Korean officials regarding NBC's coverage of the 1988 Olympics in Seoul.

The 1996 Olympics coverage was more of the same. The sports in which the United States did not excel got little coverage. Soccer is by far the most popular sport in the entire world (called "football" in most countries). Yet we saw almost none of it because the US team was eliminated early. Volleyball is far less popular than soccer. Many nations do not even enter volleyball teams in the Olympics. Yet we saw lots of volleyball because the United States had a strong team. The same held true for softball, an American-invented sport.

The networks project an image of US athletic superiority, focusing mostly on American contestants to the neglect of those from other countries, including many who might give superb performances. At the 1996 Games, in the kayaking competition we saw a premeet interview with the American Davey Hearn; we saw his girlfriend; we even saw them getting married, and we saw him through most of the race. The only trouble was, our Davey finished ninth. First place went to a Slovak, whose name flashed across the screen only for an instant. In another event, the US entry was allotted an extensive interview—without mention of the fact that he finished sixteenth. In some instances, the medal winners were never even announced if they were not Americans.

Sometimes racism wins out over nation-state chauvinism. In the triple jump, the gold medal was won by Kenny Harrison, who was American but *African* American. TV coverage instead concentrated on second-place Jonathan Edwards, a white Englishman, who happened to be a devout Christian, who talked about his gift from God to compete and how he would never compete on Sundays—until he realized he was missing out on too many important matches, then it seems God sent him a different message. The bronze medal went to a Cuban whose final jump was not even shown.

The 2000 Olympics were not much better. The scorecard ranking nations according to the number of medals won showed the United States as top medal winner. This ranking was repeatedly displayed on the screen and reproduced each day on the sports pages of just about every newspaper in the USA. Images of US gold medal winners floated across the screen again and again, some of them holding aloft giant American flags, accompanied by misty lighting, inspirational music, with all sorts of red-white-and-blue graphics in the background.

Also in 2000, US women athletes got an unusual amount of television and press coverage—mostly in those instances when they were doing better than US males. The women were competing against females from countries in which women's sports was given even less active recruitment, training, and financial support than in the United States. So we saw more of the winning US women's soccer team than of the unsuccessful US male soccer team of that year.

During that same Olympics I watched the men's volley-ball contest between China and the United States. China won the first game and was leading in the second, at which point the American announcers repeatedly com-mented on how the US team was "plagued by injuries," and had been training together "for not very long." Actually, some of the players were veterans from the pre-vious Olympics team of four years earlier; nevertheless, the announcers insisted that the team as a whole was rather green and inexperienced. In contrast, the Chinese team "has been playing together for years." That the US team was losing had to be explained away as due to a set of implicitly unfair circumstances. Then, as the US team began to catch up and went on to win the second game, the announcers stopped whining about injuries and lack of seasoning. Nor did they mention such things in the third and final game which the Americans also won, giv-ing them the match.

The International Gold Cup football (soccer) competi-tion of 2003 received zero attention in the US mainstream media until mid-July when the US team put itself in the running for the championship by beating the Cuban team 5 to 0. This particular victory was widely reported. In sports as in war, reports of US losses are minimized while US victories are shamelessly heralded as evidence of American supremacy.

☆

I like sports. I just do not like the mean-spirited competitiveness, and all the whining when losing and crass trumpeting when winning. And I have a hard time with the rabid militaristic chauvinism that too often comes with the coverage, and infects the spectators. With sports we need to foster international friendship and the more gracious side of the human spirit. Let us have less chest-thumping and more handshaking, less emphasis on who wins and more appreciation for how well the game is played by both sides. Better a family of nations than a multitude of screaming nationalistic egos.

6   THE DIVINE POLITICOS

IN THE UNITED STATES THERE IS NO SINGLE state-established church, but religion per se, as represented by the major faiths, is so closely identified with the patriotic process as to have become a kind of unofficial establishment. Opening convocations by clergymen from one or another denomination have been an essential prop for political party conventions, congressional sessions, presidential inaugurations, Thanksgiving Day dedications (a national, not a religious holiday), and a host of other patriotic gatherings. Religion in America resembles capitalism in the way it attaches itself to potent symbols beyond its own sphere: democracy, patriotism, public virtue, and the American Way of Life. "Religion and democracy go hand in hand," said Vice President Alben Barkley in 1952.[1]

With the lines between political and religious belief blurred, nonbelievers often run the risk of being labeled "un-American." Years before he became president, Richard Nixon suggested that atheists be disqualified from presidential office. In 1955, the American Legion, not the churches, launched the first "Back to God" campaign, on which occasion President Dwight Eisenhower observed, "Recognition of the Supreme Being is the first, the most basic, expression of Americanism. Without God there could be no American form of government, nor an American way of life."[2]

US leaders repeatedly weave piety with patriotism. President Nixon made it known that when he had an important decision to make regarding a moral issue, "I counsel first with Billy Graham."[3] A famous evangelical preacher, Graham was a regular visitor to the White House through several administrations. What moral dimension he actually lent to presidential decisionmaking was never made clear. Still, bringing a symbol of religiosity like Billy Graham to the White House was the next best thing to bringing God himself. It was a way of showing that the deity was on the president's side.

Another president of the *Gott mit uns* school was Ronald Reagan. A right-wing Christian organization calling itself the "Moral Majority," furnished with huge sums from reactionary tycoons, played an active role in the campaign to put him in the White House in 1981. During his eight years in office, Reagan entered into conversations with fundamentalist clergy about how the Bible prophesied a nuclear apocalypse that would destroy the Antichrist forces of godless Russians and allow Jesus to return triumphant.[4] In this scenario, God was a Cold War militarist.

On one occasion Reagan announced that the United States "is a Christian nation"—which must have come as unsettling news to the millions of loyal American Muslims, Jews, Hindus, Buddhists, atheists, agnostics, skeptics, and nonsectarian deists. In a mawkishly staged moment during his 1987 State of the Union message, Reagan cast his eyes upward as he proclaimed that our nation pays homage "to *Him*," and "could not have been created without divine guidance." God, it seems, is not just Our Father but Our Founding Father.

☆

In fact, the founders of this nation affirmed that the Republic was *not* beholden to Christianity or any other religion. Jefferson bemoaned "the impious presumption of legislators and rulers, civil as well as ecclesiastical, who . . . established and maintained false religions over the greatest part of the world."[5] James Madison wrote, "Religious bondage shackles and debilitates the mind, and unfits it for every noble enterprise, every expanded prospect."[6] The delegates to the Constitutional Convention in Philadelphia in 1787 left the deity very much out of the picture, even refusing to follow Benjamin Franklin's suggestion that their daily sessions be opened with a prayer for divine guidance.[7]

The Constitution makes clear that ours is *not* a Christian nation. Article VI reads, "no religious Test shall ever be required as a Qualification to any Office or public Trust under the United States." Edmund Randolph of Virginia, who had been a delegate to the Philadelphia Convention, hoped that the absence of a religious qualification "will prevent the establishment of any one sect in prejudice to the rest, and will forever oppose all attempts to infringe religious liberty." And George Washington maintained that "every man" should be free to worship "according to the dictates of his own conscience."[8]

Another democratic victory came with the passage of the First Amendment, which in part states: "Congress shall make no law respecting an establishment of religion or prohibiting the free exercise thereof . . ." The government could neither inhibit religious groups nor act as an agency in support of them. Church and state were to be kept separate.

☆

Every US president who goes to war enlists God as his ally. In an appearance at the Southern Baptist Convention in 1991, the elder Bush grew visibly tearful as he spoke about praying to God before ordering the attacks that massacred tens of thousands of Iraqi conscripts and civilians in the first Gulf War. During the subsequent presidential campaign, he cited Jesus Christ himself as the moral force behind US policy, claiming that "America, as Christ ordained" was "a light unto the world."[9]

At the 1992 Republican National Convention, various speakers claimed that Republicans had higher moral standards and were closer to God than Democrats.[10] One defector from the ultraright ranks, David Brock, challenged that view. In his tell-all book he revealed that any number of moralistic, family-values Republicans were guilty of infidelities, homosexual trysts, and other "scandals."[11]

The GOP's religious posturing was too much even for some religious groups. The National Council of Churches, for one, charged that it was blasphemy to make "partisan use of God's name" and "assert the moral superiority of one people over another or one political party over another." And the Baptist Joint Committee on Public Affairs announced, "We begin with the proposition that God is neither Democrat nor Republican nor, for that matter, American. God transcends all national and political affiliations."[12]

But the younger President Bush seemed to oppose the idea of a nonpartisan deity. Having recovered "with the grace of God" from the alcohol and cocaine addictions of his earlier years, he became a born-again Christian. In 1993, the year before he ran for governor of Texas, Bush provoked a small tempest by telling an Austin reporter (who happened to be Jewish) that only Jesus worshippers go to heaven. After being elevated to the US presidency by a Supreme Court vote, Bush presided over the most resolutely faith-based White House in modern times, heavily populated with Bible study groups. He attended national prayer breakfasts with greater frequency than any other president, and delivered speeches and radio broadcasts that sounded like sermons, ending with "May God continue to bless America." He also hobnobbed with the right-wing evangelist ministers who had come to occupy a central place in the Republican Party.[13]

On June 27, 2003, President Bush announced: "God told me to strike at al Qaeda and I struck them, and then he instructed me to strike at Saddam, which I did, and now I am determined to solve the problem in the Middle East."[14] *God told me? He instructed me?* Does it not become a cause for concern that the US president, sounding like an Old Testament prophet, is justifying his war policy by claiming to be in direct communication with the Almighty? It is a worrisome chain of command.

On another occasion Bush voiced his determination to "rid the world of evil" and "evildoers" even if it meant repeatedly resorting to war. It is laudable when a leader wants to help make the world a better place but somewhat disquieting when the man in the Oval Office feels he has a divine mandate to reshape the world through violent means.[15]

Pursuing policies designed to undo the separation of church and state, Bush favored prayer in the schools, opposed legal abortions, and opposed federal education programs that taught birth control and safe sex. He also supported a measure to allow churches, synagogues, and mosques to use federal funds to administer social welfare and other human services. Critics feared that the faith-based programs would replace government services for the needy but would be neither sufficiently developed nor reliably managed.[16]

Another official who saw himself as part of God's crusade on earth was the Pentagon's deputy undersecretary for intelligence, Lt. Gen. William G. Boykin. In 2003, appearing in uniform before fundamentalist Christian groups, Boykin announced that Bush "was not elected by a majority of the voters . . . he was appointed by God." Boykin charged that Islamic radicals and the North Koreans hated America "because we're . . . a nation of believers." Our "spiritual enemies will only be defeated if we come against them in the name of Jesus." Other countries, said Boykin, "have lost their morals . . . but America is still a Christian nation." Explaining how he prevailed against a Muslim militia leader in the 1993 US invasion of Somalia, Boykin proclaimed, "I knew my God was bigger than his. I knew that my God was a real God and his was an idol."[17] Apparently when God was not talking to Bush, he was talking to Boykin.

☆

The superpatriotic religionists pursue a fairly reactionary politico-economic domestic program: deregulation, privatization, elimination of publicly funded human services, an ever increasing military budget, and the like. But they also want to see the strictures of fundamentalist Christianity prevail over all aspects of American life: no separation of church and state, no abortion, no birth control, no "promiscuity," no public office for atheists, no toleration of blasphemy or "false doctrine," no homosexuality or feminism, plenty of public funds to support religious interests, Bible studies in the public schools, prayer in the classrooms, textbooks rewritten in keeping with religious credo, music and arts in a pro-Jesus idiom, so too media and movies—creeping theocracy in action.

Fundamentalist Christianity is a totalitarian system, just as it was for more than a thousand years after gaining dominance over Rome in the fourth century. Back then, the Jesus proselytes proceeded to burn all the many fine pagan libraries that existed, and destroyed forever the corpus of pagan works in philosophy, literature, history, astronomy, science, and the arts, ushering in more than a thousand oppressive years of ignorant and intolerant theocracy.[18]

In recent times, right-wing fundamentalist Randall Terry, founder of "Operation Rescue," the terroristic campaign against abortion clinics, announced that Christ worshipers have "a biblical duty to conquer this nation." He told an audience of like-minded faithful: "I want you to just let a wave of intolerance wash over you. . . . Our goal is a Christian nation. We have a Biblical duty; we are called by God to conquer this country. We don't want equal time. We don't want pluralism."[19] Were any leftist leaders to make such an encompassing proclamation about the goals of their political organizations, they would likely be roundly denounced as totalitarians, subversives, or terrorists. But Terry continued to be treated as a more or less reputable figure in public life.

As of 2004, the right-wing fundamentalist viewpoint was openly espoused by the US attorney general, the House and Senate Republican leadership, and almost 200 House representatives and senators. At the same time, the chief justice of the Supreme Court, William Rehnquist, announced: "The 'wall of separation between church and state' . . . should be frankly and explicitly abandoned."[20]

But who is controlling whom? Is there just a natural symbiosis between reactionary politicos and religious fundamentalists? Or do the fundamentalists serve a greater agenda that is choreographed by more powerful financial interests?[21] One thing is certain, as long as the religionists hew to a reactionary line, they will continue to enjoy the generous contributions provided by various right-wing moneybags.

☆

In June 2002, the US 9th Circuit Court of Appeals offered a flicker of resistance to superpatriotic religiosity by ruling that the phrase "under God," inserted into the Pledge of Allegiance by Congress in 1954, violated the First Amendment's prohibition against the establishment of a state religion. President Bush immediately supported a bill that Congress passed almost unanimously reinforcing support for the words "under God" in the pledge and for

"In God we trust" as the national motto. The Bush administration also appealed the case to the Supreme Court, arguing that reciting the Pledge of Allegiance "is a patriotic exercise, not a religious testimonial."[22] As of early 2004 God continued to maintain a place on our national coinage and in the pledges mumbled by uncomprehending children in overcrowded, underfunded classrooms.

1. *New York Times*, 15 August 1952.

2. *New York Herald Tribune*, 22 February 1955.

3. *New York Post*, 7 October 1977.

4. Peter Stiglin, "Apocalyptic Theology and the Right," *Witness*, October 1986.

5. Andrew Lipscomb, ed., *Jefferson's Works*, vol. 2 (Washington, D.C.: Thomas Jefferson Memorial Association, 1904), 223, 301.

6. Letter to William Bradford Jr., 1 April 1774, selection reprinted in Marvin Meyers, *The Mind of the Founder* (New York: Bobbs-Merrill, 1973), 6.

7. Max Farrand, ed., *The Records of the Federal Convention of 1787*, vol. 1 (New Haven: Yale University Press, 1966), 452.

8. Farrand, *Records of the Federal Convention*, vol. 3, 310; see also Madison's note regarding a religious test, ibid., vol. 2, 468; and Paul Boller Jr., *George Washington and Religion* (Dallas: Southern Methodist University Press, 1963), 88–89.

9. *New York Times*, 28 January 1992; see also *Washington Post*, 18 January 1991.

10. *San Francisco Chronicle*, 18 August 1992; *San Francisco Examiner*, 29 August 1992.

11. David Brock, *Blinded by the Right: The Conscience of an Ex-Conservative* (New York: Three Rivers Press, 2002), passim.

12. Excerpts from all three statements can be found in the *New York Times*, 30 August 1992.

13. Martin E. Marty, "The Sin of Pride," *Newsweek*, 10 March 2003.

14. Bush quoted in D. F. Florentino, *Reign of Error* (Burlington, Vermont: Toward Freedom, 2004), 39.

15. Karen Yourish, "Delivering the 'Good News,'" *Newsweek*, 10 March 2003; Marty, "The Sin of Pride"; and "Bush's Messiah Complex," *Progressive*, February 2003.

16. Howard Fineman, "Bush and God," *Newsweek*, 10 March 2003; and Elisabeth Bumiller, "Anti-War Clerics Find Access to Bush Barred," *International Herald Tribune*, 11 March 2003.

17. *Los Angeles Times*, 16 October 2003; see also *Washington Post*, 22 October 2003.

18. On the Christian suppression of Western Civilization, see my *History as Mystery* (San Francisco: City Lights Books, 1999), chapters 2 and 3.

19. Quoted in Kimberly Blaker, ed., *The Fundamentals of Extremism: The Christian Right in America* (New Boston, Michigan: New Boston Books, 2003), 25; also Theodore Roszak, "The One Right Way," *San Francisco Chronicle Magazine*, 13 July 2003.

20. Quoted in Blaker, *The Fundamentals of Extremism*, 154.

21. Question posed by Gilles d'Aymery, in HYPERLINK "http://www.swans.com/library/art9/ga158.html" www.swans.com/library/art9/ga158.html, 7 July 2003.

22. *Elk Grove Unified School District vs. Newdow* (2004).

7   MESSIANIC NATION

THE IDEA THAT THE UNITED STATES WAS intended by God, history, or destiny to play a unique and superior role in the world gathered strength early in our history as national consciousness took hold. "The hand of Divinity itself" shapes the nation's destiny, according to a youthful Alexander Hamilton. And John Adams intoned, "Our pure, virtuous, public spirited, federative republic will last forever, govern the globe and introduce the perfection of man." From the earliest days of the Republic, orators dwelled on America's beauty, abundance, and, above all, its promise of material progress. In 1845, the *United States Journal* rhapsodized, "[All] the channels of communication, public and private, through the school-room, the pulpit, and the press—are engrossed and occupied with this one idea, which all these forces are combined to disseminate: that we the American people are the most independent, intelligent, moral, and happy people on the face of the earth."[1]

Such a conviction prevails to this day. In 2002, a prominent right-wing publication, asserted that "our country has, with all our mistakes and blunders, always been and always will be the greatest beacon of freedom, charity, opportunity, and affection in history."[2] But the superpatriotic dedication to freedom has been honored more in the breach. This was evident during the early Cold War era when opinion polls indicated that some 97 percent of Americans believed in the superiority of democracy and the right to free speech, but over two out of three would refuse a Communist the right to speak, and almost the same proportion would deprive an atheist of a public platform.[3] We might recall the celebrated writer and humorist, Mark Twain, who once said that the three most precious things Americans possess are "freedom of speech, freedom of conscience, and the prudence never to practice either."

Nationalistic devotion tends to mimic religious devotion, not only in its intolerance of dissent but in its very forms and belief structure. Like the church, the nation-state has its inspirational myths of sacred genesis and apocalyptic crises; its early prophets and martyrs; its sacred dogma, rituals, symbols, monuments, and hymns; its parchments engrossed with the revealed word; its devotional pledges uttered like prayers; and its commemorative holidays and convocations.

☆

At the core of a nation's devotional message is its claim to playing a uniquely ordained role in the world. In 2003 President George W. Bush announced that the United States was unique in that it was doing God's work on earth, bringing God's gift of liberty to "every human being in the world."[4] To be sure, the United States does have a unique history, but so do many other nations with their extraordinary annals, filled with epic social struggles, unusual ethnic mixes, international clashes, inspiring achievements, hopeful visions, and horrific political crimes and atrocities. And the nationalists of other countries have claimed a unique messianic mission for their respective peoples— much as our superpatriotic leaders do for the United States. If anything, Americans are rather unexceptional in thinking that theirs is an exceptional nation.

Start with the Old Testament itself, with its asseveration that the Israelites were God's Chosen People, doing Jehovah's bidding, serving as his exemplary acolytes here on earth as they leveled whole cities of heathens and non-believers. Indeed, there is no bloodier compendium of nationalistic carnage and messianic atrocity than the Old Testament.

Then there were the leaders of the Roman Empire and, centuries later, the British Empire, who had nothing critical to say about imperial plunder and exploitation and instead spoke of conquest as a grandly civilizing accomplishment, an uplifting expedition that brought unity, peace, and happiness to the colonized peoples.

Among the various nineteenth-century nationalist movements was the Indian National Congress, which propagated a vision of India as fulfilling the unique historic task of guiding humankind toward a redeeming path. Endowed with a rich and ancient spiritual tradition, India would save Europe from its competitive strife and its crass and superficial materialism. The Indian patriots sermonized their youth: "You shall help to create a nation, to spiritualize an epoch, to Aryanize the world. And that nation is your own, that epoch belongs to you and your children, and that world is no mere tract of land, but the whole earth with its teeming millions."[5]

At about that same time in France, Jules Michelet was putting forth a messianic message: The French Revolution had given humanity the great gift of liberty, equality, and national self-realization, with France itself now "the glorious pilot of mankind's ship." France's unique mission was not only the deliverance of its own citizenry but of all other peoples. *La belle France* was the great amphitheater in which ideas and arts assumed world importance and radiated everywhere. Upon France depended the world's salvation, the climax and fulfillment of human history itself.[6]

If France had Michelet, Italy at the threshold of its unification had Vincenzo Gioberti and, more important,

Giuseppe Mazzini, both of whom proclaimed the moral and historic primacy of the Italians. "Italy is the chosen people, the typical people, the creative people, the Israel of the modern age,"[7] declared Gioberti. With even greater fervor, Mazzini saw in the emergence of a newly united Italian nation the instrument for the regeneration of all humanity. Italy had served as the "center of civilization" twice before, under the Roman Empire and later under the Roman Church. With its long delayed *Risorgimento*, Mazzini went on, Italy would emerge afresh in the modern age "to unite the world," this time advancing the cause of freedom, peace, and democracy.[8]

Less benign than Michelet and Mazzini were German nationalists such as Johan Fichte and Heinrich von Treitschke, who believed that Germany was destined to conquer and expand in accordance with the natural laws of history, not by using democracy and parliamentary rule but with *Macht*, with sheer power exercised by a strong monarch and a victorious army. And this would benefit everyone, for Germany—with its nobility of soul, intellectual preeminence, and martial strength—would lead the world away from the degenerating effects of liberalism, materialism, equality, and individualism.[9]

Consider also the messianic Pan-Slavs and Russian supernationalists, most notably the great novelist Fyodor Dostoevsky, who held forth about the "Russian soul." According to Dostoevsky, the Russians possessed a deep intuitive grasp of life and a deep God-bearing orthodox devotion that was lacking in the decadent Western nations. Russia would unite all the Slav peoples not for the sake of empire but to ensure their peace and well-being. Holy Mother Russia was destined to become the arbiter and ruler of humankind, revealing to the rest of Europe a new social order that she alone embodied.[10]

So into the twentieth century, the hypernationalists and imperialists of Nazi Germany and fascist Japan put forth their "unique" visions of moral regeneration, nationalist supremacy, racial purification, and world domination.

To repeat, the one certain thing about the US superpatriots' claim to messianic exceptionalism is how strikingly *un*exceptional and *un*original it really is. Throughout history any number of other movements, nations, and empires have thought of themselves as God's gift to humanity. Captivated by their own Chosen People mythology, they believed they alone were preeminently qualified to lead the world—much as the present-day proponents of a global American empire.

☆

The messianic impulse is compounded when national virtue is wedded to extraordinary military power. The superpatriots see evidence of their divine calling in the very power that enables them to thrust themselves into every corner of the world. The contention that "we must mobilize our power in order to lead" soon becomes "we must lead because we are so powerful." It might do us well to recall the counsel afforded by Senator William Fulbright in 1966: "We are not God's chosen savior of mankind but only one of mankind's more successful and fortunate branches, endowed by our Creator with about the same capacity for good and evil, no more or less, than the rest of humanity."[11]

Almost forty years later, a news columnist, Jon Carroll, put it even more emphatically: "We are not the only democracy in the world; we are not the only country that exhibits courage in the face of adversity. We lie and cheat and steal and murder. Any assumption that God conferred on us a special blessing is not backed up by the facts. We fail to sign international treaties, and we reserve the right to violate such treaties whenever we feel like it. Is that because God speaks to our leaders as he speaks to no others?"[12]

The peoples of other nations are understandably reluctant to accept the messianic view of the United States as the all-knowing world leader. International surveys reveal that they see the United States as "arrogant, aggressive, and self-absorbed." Large majorities in various countries are distrustful of US leaders and strongly disapprove of US military invasions, such as the one launched against Iraq in 2003. And they keenly feel that Washington's policies have a deleterious effect on their own countries.[13]

A survey conducted by *New York Times* correspondents around the world in 2003 found a widespread opinion of the United States as "an imperial power that has defied world opinion through unjustified and unilateral use of military force," bent on "controlling global oil supplies and on military domination."[14] Unfortunately, such negative responses only convince our superpatriotic leaders and media pundits that we need to project our image more effectively so that other peoples will have a clearer appreciation of America's virtuous intentions. In effect, the superpatriots are saying that when foreigners challenge US policies, this should lead us to question *their* judgment, not our own, certainly not the policies that evoke such negative responses.

☆

Messianic nationalistic morality is an inversion of individual morality. Ordinarily we might think of the nation-state as an instrument of social organization whose function is to protect the interests of its populace. For the superpatriot, however, the nation-state is not just a legal unit of rule, with contractual rights and obligations; it is a kind of living entity that offers its citizens meaningful direction and moral regeneration. The nation becomes something of an end in itself, a powerful Absolute that claims our ultimate loyalty, whose existence and survival is taken as self-justifying, beyond the reach of moral criticism.

The ethical code applied to nationalism does not operate like the one pertaining to individuals. Individual morality calls for self-restraint and even self-sacrifice. There are certain things one should not do (as in "thou shalt not") even if one has the impulse and even if it serves one's pleasure or advances one's self-interest. Individual morality is predicated on the realization that sin (that is, unjust and harmful behavior toward others) is always within the human potential. To err is human, to sin is all too human. But these premises are inverted when applied to a nation's behavior, for the nation-state is something more than human.

At the heart of the secular religion of nationalism rests the belief that the messianic nation's existence and its action are so endowed with virtue as to place it beyond the commonplace rules that govern individual morality. As a kind of supreme entity, the nation knows no restraint other than what is imposed by the limitations of its own desires and power. The most ruthless violence—insupportable in civil society—is applauded as heroism when performed in the name of the nation.[15] "Thou shalt not" becomes "Thou shalt do anything by whatever means necessary if it can be said to be in the national interest." Ergo, the willingness to kill other human beings in combat is treated not only as morally acceptable but as a heroic measure of one's patriotism. Instead of going to jail, the perpetrators are honored with medals and ceremonial acclaim.

The inverted morality of superpatriotism demands that a nation have not only a right but a duty to do whatever it deems necessary to protect its own security. While the end is laudable, one might question the blanket mandate. Since "national security" is as difficult to define as the dangers that might threaten it, the tendency is to equate the barely possible with the almost certain, the remote conflict with the imminent threat, the imaginable with the inevitable. Thus, homeland security and national self-defense are interpreted not merely as defense against actual or impending attack but against anything imaginable that might possibly infringe upon US security. One can never be too sure, so let's arrest the whole lot of them here at home, and bomb the hell out of them abroad. US security, in turn, is seen as requiring the expansion of US influence into every corner of the world, with military force being applied in whatever way the president so chooses.

"Why is it that, no matter what the cost to another nation or to international society, the right of preserving the nation and all its vital interests is considered morally unquestionable?" asked Albert Weinberg over sixty years ago.[16] Were we ever to ponder that question we might decide that there are some actions that—even if deemed vital for preserving some vaguely defined "US interests"— are so morally reprehensible as to be eschewed.

We might further wonder whether the limitless pursuit of national security does not itself become self-defeating. If doing "whatever we judge fit to maintain our security" necessitates wreaking death and destruction on other nations, this can have terrible repercussions for our own country. The result is that the nation most obsessed with "organizing the peace" and "propagating democracy" and "uplifting the world" is the one that propagates autocratic control and ends up entangled in perpetual war.

Messianic nationalism is the path down which a nation can lose its soul.

1. Editorial, *United States Journal*, 18 October 1845.
2. Larry Miller, "You Say You Want a Resolution," *Weekly Standard*, 14 January 2002.
3. Samuel Stouffer, *Communism, Conformity and Civil Liberties* (Garden City, N.Y.: Doubleday, 1955), 29–42.
4. Howard Fineman, "Bush and God," *Newsweek*, 10 March 2003.
5. Quoted in Hans Kohn, *Prophets and Peoples* (New York: Collier Books, 1961, originally published 1946), 15.
6. Kohn, *Prophets and Peoples*, 52–53; see also Jean-Marie Carré, *Michelet et son Temps* (Paris: Perrin 1926).
7. Quoted in Kohn, *Prophets and Peoples*, 79.
8. Giuseppe Mazzini, *The Duties of Man and other Essays* (New York: Everyman's Library 1961). On both Mazzini and Gioberti, see Giovanni Faldella, *Profeti Massimi* (Turino: Lattes, 1910), chapters 1–3 and passim.
9. Kohn, *Prophets and Peoples*, chapter 4.
10. Kohn, *Prophets and Peoples*, 139–40 and passim.
11. J. William Fulbright, *The Arrogance of Power* (New York: Random House, 1966), 20.
12. *San Francisco Chronicle*, 3 July 2003.
13. See, for instance, survey reports of the Pew Research Center for the People and the Press, March 2003.
14. *New York Times*, 11 September 2003.
15. See Albert K. Weinberg, *Manifest Destiny* (Chicago: Quadrangle Books, 1935).
16. Weinberg, *Manifest Destiny*, 410.

8   FOLLOW THE LEADER

THE DISTINCT CHARACTERISTIC OF THE state, said German sociologist Max Weber, is that it alone claims a "monopoly of the legitimate use of physical force within a given territory."[1] The state's irreducible essence rests in its capacity to wield legally defined violence against its own citizens. In many instances, the target is not just the criminal element but also political dissenters who challenge the existing distribution of privilege, wealth, institutional authority, and ideological orthodoxy.

Laws dealing with sedition and terrorism are enlisted against troublesome dissidents, but so is the ordinary criminal code: disorderly conduct, mob action, criminal trespass, destruction of property, felonious assault, resisting arrest, and the like. In this way, acts of dissent and protest are both depoliticized and criminalized by the repressive operations carried out by state authorities.

State power is wielded primarily by the executive, specifically the president and the national security apparatus. Representing the entire nation rather than a particular locale, the president "possesses a sort of divine right," as Marx noted of the French presidency in the Second Republic in 1852. "He is the elect of the nation" who stands "in a personal relation to the nation." Through its individual representatives the National Assembly exhibits manifold aspects of the nation, but in the president the "national spirit finds its incarnation."[2]

The US Constitution gives Congress, not the president, the power to make war. Yet again and again US forces are committed to military actions by presidential order, without a declaration of war. Indeed, some presidents make a point of ignoring Congress on this matter. In late 1990, while the legislators debated whether the United States should engage in hostilities against Iraq, President Bush *père* went on record as saying, "I don't care if I get one vote in Congress. We're going in."[3] Bush understood that during times of crisis and national peril—real or fabricated— Congress would not dare impeach the commander-in-chief for such a trifle as an undeclared war, especially since so many of the lawmakers were themselves fervent superpatriotic militarists.

Presidential usurpation of the warmaking power took a final giant step in the aftermath of the September 2001 terrorist attacks that destroyed the twin towers of the World Trade Center in New York and a wing of the Pentagon, with the loss of some 3,000 lives. Congress voted outright to give the president the power to decide when the nation should go to war. This surrender of congressional power to the executive was itself an unconstitutional forfeiture. In effect, Bush *fils* could now unilaterally declare war whenever he wanted, a one-man decisionmaking power usually enjoyed only by absolute monarchs and dictators.

And when Bush exercised that unconstitutional power by going to war against Iraq in March 2003, in the face of worldwide protests, the great majority of congressional lawmakers, out of fear of seeming unpatriotic, fell into line, including many who had initially opposed the war as ill-conceived and illicit. Thus Democratic leader of the House of Representatives, Nancy Pelosi (D-Calif.), speaking as if she were in the US Army rather than in the US Congress, announced that now that our troops were committed to action, we had to support our commander-in-chief. "I support the president. . . . We are one team in one fight, and we stand together," she proclaimed.[4]

☆

Some of our citizens are understandably cynical and suspicious about politics. Politicians, we hear, cannot be trusted; they are often corrupt and self-serving, saying one thing during election campaigns, then doing something else once they get into office. All true enough. Yet these same citizens display an almost childlike trust and knee-jerk faith when politicians trumpet a need to defend our national security. So it happens that with the launching of each new US war against one or another small but "menacing" nation, superpatriots rally around the flag, draped as it is around the president. The nation is under siege from a lethal foreign threat, we are told. This is no time for splitting hairs about right and wrong. Get behind our president and our nation; support our troops; destroy the alien menace. When he claims to serve the higher good, the commander-in-chief can do no wrong. The inverted morality is activated.

We should remind ourselves of what happened in Germany in the 1930s when Hitler and his Nazi thugs took power (financed by the big moneyed cartels). The Nazis insisted that unquestioning obedience and adulation be accorded the leader. It was governance by *der Feuhrerprinzip*, the leader principle, the notion that the head of state is the living embodiment of the state itself, the supreme repository of the nation's virtues. It is a short step from the cult of the nation (superpatriotism) to the cult of the leader. In the case of Nazi Germany, the world reaped bitter fruit.

To those who say that during times of crisis we must have faith in the president, we might ask: *Faith?* Is this religion or politics? Is the president to be treated as an object of worship? We are told we must trust the president, but what does that mean? Trust is something we extend to loved ones or very close friends and family (and even then, check them out once in a while). Democracy is not about trust; it is about *distrust*. It is about accountability, exposure, open debate, critical challenge, and popular input and feedback from the citizenry. It is about responsible government. We have to get our fellow Americans to trust their leaders less and themselves more, trust their own questions and suspicions, and their own desire to know what is going on.

There is nothing like a war or a major crisis to reduce adult citizens to mindless conformity, ready to play "follow the leader" out of a perceived need for national unity and a hope that our *Reichführer*, the president, will see us through the danger. President Franklin Roosevelt's highest rating, 84 percent, came immediately after the Japanese attacked Pearl Harbor in 1941. President John Kennedy's 83 percent approval rating came after his 1961 Bay of Pigs invasion of Cuba, even though the operation failed. And after the Gulf War of 1991, the elder Bush's approval rating zoomed to 93 percent.[5]

☆

Consider the case of George Bush the younger. War and violence were especially good to this president. As of 10 September 2001, his presidency was floundering and his approval ratings were sagging woefully. Then the next day came the attacks on the World Trade Center and the

Pentagon, and Bush saw his rating leap up to 82 percent. This was swiftly followed by his newly trumpeted "permanent war against terrorism" and the massive bombing and invasion of Afghanistan. Bush was transmuted into the determined leader who would rally the nation, shore up our defenses (or certainly our defense *budget*) with ever larger military allocations, and protect us with legislation that strengthened the repressive powers of the federal executive.

Here was the president protecting us from threats at home and abroad, addressing military gatherings, flying onto aircraft carriers for photo opportunities—unmindful of how in earlier years he himself had been AWOL from his duties in the Air National Guard and arguably was a deserter. Standing proudly in front of the cameras, with a steely gaze fixed on the nation's ramparts, ready to move decisively against any and all, never did this corrupt but affable draft-dodging Jesus-freak billionaire and former cokehead alcoholic seem so *presidential*. His approval ratings skyrocketed.

Then came the corporate scandals of the spring and summer of 2002, the Enron, WorldCom, Harkin, and Halliburton investment crimes. By July, both President Bush and Vice-President Dick Cheney were directly implicated in fraudulent insider trading practices. Their respective companies, Harkin and Halliburton, made false accounting claims of profit to pump up stock values. Bush and Cheney, along with other company officers and top investors, armed with insider information about when to get out, sold their stock at prime value just before it was revealed to be nearly worthless and collapsed in price. Both the president and vice-president made dubious statements about what they knew and did not know. They refused to hand over documents and gave every appearance of being directly implicated in deceptive practices that cost smaller investors billions of dollars.

By July 2002, the Republican Party was reeling from the insider-trading scandals and was pegged as the party of corporate favoritism and corruption. But by September, with war pending against Iraq, the GOP reemerged as the party of patriotism, national defense, and strong military leadership to gain control of both houses of Congress, winning elections it might not otherwise have won. The impending war blew the whole Enron-Harkin-Halliburton scandal off the front pages and out of the evening news. Instead of being subjected to criminal investigation and impeachment, Bush, the insider trader, remained untouched in the White House, reemerging as our fearless peerless wartime leader.

☆

The elder Bush had done the same thing in 1990–1991. In late 1990, his popularity was slumping badly because of the savings and loan scandal. Every evening, TV news programs were peeling off successive layers of corruption, thievery, bribery, and plunder of the public treasury, in what was the greatest financial conspiracy in the history of the world, involving a raid of the public treasury that has come to over $1 trillion. Two and possibly three of Bush's sons risked going to jail for financial legerdemain. But once Bush launched the first Gulf War against Iraq, the networks became preoccupied with selling that war, and the savings and loan issue was blown out of the evening news and sent into media limbo. The Gulf victory also made it harder to investigate disclosures implicating Bush senior himself in the Iran-contra conspiracy, as he basked in what seemed like an untouchable popularity.

There is no guarantee that such popularity will last. As mentioned earlier, Bush senior's approval rating after the Gulf War was at 93 percent. Yet the following year he lost the presidency to a garrulous governor from Arkansas. So with the younger Bush. His ratings began to sag in the winter of 2002–2003 as the terrorism hype subsided and the economy remained in the doldrums. By 14 March 2003, his approval rating was at 53 percent. But on 18 March, after he began war operations against Iraq, Bush's ratings climbed to 68 percent.[6] By late April, with a swift and easy military victory seemingly at hand, he was once more over 80 percent.

In the months that followed, Bush II continued to play the terrorism card. Within a brief span of several weeks in September 2003, he referred to terrorist dangers when talking about (a) the war in Iraq, (b) energy policy, (c) the state of the economy, and (d) US dealings with the United

Nations. Such persistent references to terrorism were designed to discourage criticism and keep the public rallied behind his leadership. But then, as the "liberation" of Iraq devolved into a protracted people's resistance that proved costly in American lives and dollars, this strategy no longer played as well, and Bush's ratings slumped decisively.

In sum, the executive mantle of militaristic patriotism makes it easy for US presidents to gain quick—but not necessarily durable—popularity. In turn, this follow-the-leader popularity allows them to deliver the nation into wars of aggression that arguably serve none of the people's needs. But on some occasions, when the military ventures prove too costly, Americans begin to balk and show signs of disaffection.

1. Max Weber, "Politics as a Vocation," in Hans Gerth and C. Wright Mills, eds., *From Max Weber: Essays in Sociology* (New York: Oxford University Press, 1958), 78. Weber recognized that the right to apply force is sometimes allotted to nongovernmental institutions—as with security guards and private police—but "only to the extent to which the state permits it."

2. Karl Marx, "The Eighteenth Brumaire of Louis Bonaparte" in *Selected Works*, vol. 1 (Moscow: Progress Publishers, 1969), 411.

3. Richard Ben Cramer, "Bush Is Down. Now Watch Out," *New York Times*, 18 August 1992.

4. Quoted in Norman Solomon, "Pelosi's Bridge Too Far," *San Francisco Bay Guardian*, 14 January 2004.

5. Ron Faucheaux, cited in Sheldon Rampton and John Stauber, *Weapons of Mass Deception* (New York: Jeremy Tarcher/Penguin, 2003), 144.

6. Faucheaux in Rampton and Stauber, *Weapons of Mass Deception*.

9   PATRIOTIC FEAR

SUPERPATRIOTS CAN BE FOUND IN HIGH and not so high places, in the White House and the local American Legion post. We have been taught to think of blue-collar macho caricatures such as Joe Six-Pack, Tony Hardhat, and Clyde Redneck as the hypernationalist prototypes. In fact, working Americans are less the promoters of superpatriotism and more its consumers and victims. They pay the heavy taxes that support a US global military empire. They suffer the cuts in human services when so much of the nation's treasure is dissipated on war. And be they modest-income whites, African Americans, Latinos, Asians, or whomever—they provide the foot soldiers who sacrifice life and limb in the empire's military ventures.

It is the *politico-economic rulers* of this polity who are the major progenitors of superpatriotic ideology. They play a crucial role in what Cecilia O'Leary calls "managing rituals of mass allegiance."[1] They promote flag reverence, loyalty oaths, and nationalistic anniversaries. They urge the teaching of a sanitized version of US history in public schools, and establish national shrines and monuments. And they inaugurate the intensive propaganda campaigns that depict one or another foreign leader, nation, or movement as a threat to our national security. Patriotic pride is not enough. They know that a surer way to rally support for their ventures abroad is by inciting alarm at home. Behind all the patriotic cheer there lurks a heavy dose of patriotic fear.

☆

Consider the witch hunts that were conducted against the "Red Menace" for the better part of the twentieth century. Of their own accord the American people supposedly were seized by a national hysteria, a collective phobia that caused them to see demon Communists lurking everywhere. In fact, the public's fear of Communism was tirelessly propagated over the years by federal and state authorities, corporate heads, media moguls, educational administrators, and other public and private elites.

If anyone was immediately fear stricken by the emergence of Communism, it was the moneyed classes of the world. The plutocrats of various capitalist nations greeted the Russian Revolution of 1917 as a nightmare come true. The workers and peasants had overthrown not only the autocratic czar but the rich propertied class that owned the factories, mineral resources, and most of the lands of the czarist empire. As US secretary of state Robert Lansing noted at the time, the Russian Revolution served as a dangerous share-the-wealth example to the common people of other nations, including Americans, encouraging them to acquire through political means that which can only be achieved through hard work and diligence.[2]

In 1918, the United States—along with England, France, Canada, and ten other capitalist countries—invaded Soviet Russia as part of a devastating but unsuccessful attempt to destroy the revolutionary Bolshevik (Communist) government, a chapter of history unknown to most Americans. The common people of these Western nations expressed no great demand for military intercession into Soviet Russia. Quite the contrary; after a sanguinary world war that had just taken millions of lives, most people in the West wanted nothing more of bloodletting. The armed expedition to overthrow the Bolsheviks was hatched by their rulers without any public debate.

During the same years, ruling authorities in the United States set about alerting the populace to the "Red Menace." US congressional investigations produced witnesses who gave harrowing accounts of the horrors of Communist revolution in Russia. As one historian describes it:

> These witnesses declared that the Red Army was composed mainly of criminals, that the Russian

Revolution had been conducted largely by former East-Side New York Jews, that Bolshevism was the AntiChrist, and that a stronger policy of allied intervention was necessary. Ambassador Francis . . . maintained that the Bolsheviki were killing everybody "who wears a white collar or who is educated and who is not a Bolshevik. . . ."

Anti-Bolshevik testimony was played up in the columns of the nation's newspapers and once again the reading public was fed on highly colored tales of free love, nationalization of women, bloody massacres, and brutal atrocities. . . . Newspaper editors never tired of referring to the Russian Reds as "assassins and madmen," "human scum," "crime-mad," and "beasts." . . . Newspapers climaxed this sensational reporting with gigantic headlines: RED PERIL HERE, PLAN BLOODY REVOLUTION, and WANT WASHINGTON GOVERNMENT OVERTURNED.[3]

After World War I, US attorney general Mitchell Palmer conducted raids against radical organizations, publications, and labor unions, incarcerating political dissidents on trumped-up sedition charges, and deporting hundreds of immigrants charged with publicly entertaining anticapitalist notions.

Anticommunist witch hunts gathered renewed steam after World War II. Both governmental and private employees—from physicists to prize fighters—had their personal lives and opinions scrutinized by federal, state, and local authorities. Thousands of law-abiding persons were purged from academia and from private industry because of their iconoclastic views or affiliations to organizations that were opposed to free-market corporate capitalism. Millions were required to sign loyalty oaths. Prosecutions under the Smith Act and state sedition trials during the 1950s, followed by trumped-up prosecutions of student peace activists and Black militants during the sixties and seventies, gave the United States a growing number of political prisoners.[4]

The overthrow of the Soviet Union and other Eastern European Communist states from 1989 to 1992 did not bring much relief from anticommunist hype. Today, articles, books, films, and other preachments against communism continue to be produced, if not with quite the same abundance, certainly with the same demonizing certitude. Anticommunism continues to be inextricably linked to patriotism, while patriotism is wedded to "American free enterprise," the whole comprising something called "free-market democracy." Persons and organizations interested in developing more equitable and communal economic arrangements are seen as tainted by alien ideologies and wanting in loyalty to their country.

Anticommunist orthodoxy so permeates US political culture that some eminent progressive intellectuals are still denouncing the now defunct Soviet Union, while pointing accusatory fingers at the shadowy ghost of

"Stalinism," which they see lurking within the progressive community. This Left anticommunism matches anything found on the political Right in its knee-jerk persistence.[5]

☆

For decades various US rulers claimed that a huge military budget and repeated US interventions around the world were necessary to contain an expansionist world Communist movement with its headquarters in Moscow (or sometimes Beijing). But after the overthrow of the Soviet Union and other Eastern European Communist nations, Washington made no move to diminish its military spending. Cold War weapons programs proceeded in full force, with new ones being added all the time, including elaborate plans to militarize outer space. To justify this continued global military apparatus, the White House and Pentagon began issuing jeremiads about a host of new enemies who menaced the USA, mostly smaller remote countries that were vastly weaker than the United States.

The American people do not usually clamor for war or leap eagerly into armed conflict. Many will support an overseas military invasion once it is launched, but they do not of themselves urge such undertakings. They initiate many *anti*-war demonstrations but few if any *pro*-war ones. There are no vast crowds taking to the streets demanding that we bomb Iraq, invade Panama, dismember Yugoslavia, or spend another twenty years in Indochina. When they do lend support to military intervention, it is usually because they have been frightened into believing it is a matter of their very security and survival.

Listen to what one key member of the US policy elite had to say: John Foster Dulles was a wealthy corporate lawyer, conservative Republican, and secretary of state in the Eisenhower administration. (His brother and fellow multimillionaire, Allen Dulles, served as CIA director.) John Foster was keenly aware of the need to stoke popular fears: "In order to bring a nation to support the burdens of maintaining great military establishments, it is necessary to create an emotional state akin to war psychology. *There must be the portrayal of external menace*" [my italics]. To achieve this, Dulles went on, it is necessary to depict one's own country as a shining hero and the other country as the vilest villain. Once such an ideology has been fostered, the nation is "a long way on the path to war."[6]

Nazi leader Hermann Goering offered a similar estimate when interviewed during the Nuremberg war crimes trials:

> Why of course the *people* don't want war. Why should some poor slob on a farm want to risk his life in a war when the best that he can get out of it is to come back to his farm in one piece? Naturally, the common people don't want war; neither in Russia nor in England nor in America, nor for that matter in Germany. That is understood. But after all it is the *leaders* of the country who determine the policy and it is always a simple matter to drag the people

along. . . . [T]he people can always be brought to the
bidding of the leaders. That is easy. All you have to
do is tell them they are being attacked and denounce
the pacifists for lack of patriotism and exposing the
country to danger. It works the same way in any
country.[7]

With each newly minted crisis, US leaders roll out the
same time-tested scenario. They start demonizing a foreign leader (or leadership group), charging them with
being communistic or otherwise dictatorial, dangerously
aggressive, power hungry, genocidal, given to terrorism or
drug trafficking, ready to deny us access to vital resources,
harboring weapons of mass destruction, or just inexplica-
bly "anti-American" and "anti-West." Lacking any information to the contrary, the frightened public, just as
Goering said, are swept along.

☆

There is nothing particularly original in this intervention-
ist scenario. It has been used for generations, most
recently against Allende in Chile, Qaddafi in Libya, the
New Jewel movement in Grenada, Noriega in Panama, the
Sandinistas in Nicaragua, Milosevic in Yugoslavia, the
FARC guerrillas in Colombia, the Soviet-support revolutionary government in Afghanistan, Chavez in Venezuela,
Aristide in Haiti, and Saddam in Iraq (who truly was an
oppressor but one whom the US previously had supported

for years). And once the leader is designated an evil menace and his country a rogue state, then US leaders claim license to undermine that country's government with sanctions, trade embargoes, economic sabotage, subversive destabilization, mercenary paramilitaries, or if necessary direct aerial attacks and invasion by US forces.

Consider how a war psychology was generated to support the Gulf War against Iraq in early 1991. Despite all the jingoistic hype put out by the White House and the news media in the summer and autumn of 1990, support for military action against Iraq remained lukewarm at best, with a majority of Americans holding out for a diplomatic solution, specifically a peaceful withdrawal of Iraqi troops from Kuwait. The Iraqis themselves were offering to withdraw, while calling for a Middle East peace conference to settle disputes, an offer that Washington ignored.

Then, one opinion poll asked people if they would support an attack on Iraq to prevent that country from developing a "nuclear capability" (the term "weapons of mass destruction" having not yet come into vogue). Over 70 percent answered affirmatively. Immediately afterward, the elder Bush began insisting that Iraq posed a *nuclear* threat to the USA. The bloody tyrant Saddam, who would stop at nothing and who was "worse than Hitler," as the president himself exclaimed, had to be stopped from blowing us all up.[8] Public opinion began to shift in favor of intervention.

Twelve years later, the fear formula was applied anew, with Iraq again the designated menace. This time it was the younger Bush who repeatedly stated that Saddam's weapons of mass destruction posed "a serious and mounting threat to our nation" with consequences that would be "grave and tragic" if we failed to act. The Iraqi regime possessed "a vast arsenal of deadly biological and chemical weapons." "We cannot wait for final proof, the smoking gun," he argued. "It could come in the form of a mushroom cloud."9

Chief UN arms inspector Hans Blix remarked that the White House maintained a 100 percent certainty that Iraqi weapons of mass destruction existed—based on zero percent evidence. It did not go unnoticed that no weapons of mass destruction, no nuclear missiles or chemical and biological arms, were used by Iraq during the war and none could be found by US occupational forces after the war. In January 2004, an exhaustive study produced by the nonpartisan Carnegie Endowment for International Peace found that the Bush administration had "systematically misrepresented" the threat from Iraq's weapons program. The White House, the study concluded, had conjured an imaginary scenario that had no basis in actual intelligence reports.

The president and major media fabricated another frightening claim: Saddam Hussein was working hand in glove with the al Qaeda terrorists.10 But US intelligence agencies produced no evidence to support this charge. During closed sessions with a House committee, White House officials themselves were asked several times whether they had any proof that the Iraqi government was collaborating with Islamic terrorist organizations. They unequivocally stated that no such link could be found.[11]

Yet, by late 2003, well after Iraq had been occupied by US forces, a majority of Americans—especially those who got their news from the more ideologically driven Fox network—still believed one or more of these three assertions: that Iraq was linked to al Qaeda, that weapons of mass destruction had been found, and that world opinion favored the US invasion of Iraq—all untrue.[12] Once fear takes hold, evidence becomes largely irrelevant.

1. O'Leary, *To Die For*, 221.

2. See Lansing's comments quoted in William Appleman Williams, "American Intervention in Russia: 1917–1920," in David Horowitz, ed., *Containment and Revolution* (Boston: Beacon Press, 1967), 38.

3. Robert K. Murray, *Red Scare* (New York: McGraw-Hill, 1955), 95–98.

4. Preston, *Aliens and Dissenters;* and David Caute, *The Great Fear* (New York: Simon and Schuster, 1978); and my *Democracy for the Few*, chapter 10. On the murderous repression of the Black Panther Party, see Mumia Abu-Jamal, *We Want Freedom* (Cambridge: Mass., South End Press, 2004).

5. For a more extended discussion of Left anticommunism, see my *Blackshirts and Reds: Rational Fascism and the Overthrow of Communism* (San Francsico: City Lights, 1997), chapter 3.

6. Quoted in Norman Cousins, "Unremembered History," *Los Angeles Times Book Review*, 1 February 1987.

7. Quoted in Gustave Gilbert, *Nuremberg Diary* (New York: Farrar, Straus, 1947), 278–79.

8. The pretexts for the 1991 Gulf War are treated in more detail in my *Against Empire*, 100–104.

9. See Bush's statement before the United Nations, 7 February 2003; also clips of him on PBS, *Frontline*, 22 January 2004; and in *Uncovered: The Whole Truth About the Iraq War*, a documentary produced and directed by Robert Greenwald.

10. *New York Times*, 7 September 2003.

11. *San Francisco Chronicle*, 20 September 2002.

12. See Deck Deckert, "More Is Less," Swans, 3 November 2003 <www.swans.com/library/art9/rdeck046.html>.

10   THE MENACE FROM WITHIN

THROUGH MUCH OF OUR HISTORY WE have been warned about this or that alien peril. But the perceived threat does not always come from abroad. Throughout much of the nineteenth and early twentieth centuries, the business-owned press stoked an antiradical hysteria among the general public by targeting the "dangerous classes" within the USA itself, specifically the poor, the underemployed, and anyone who organized for decent paying jobs and better work conditions. Labor agitation was stigmatized as a menace to the American Way of Life.

True Americanism was equated with an uncritical acceptance of the corporate business system. "Industrialists joined publishers in branding labor activists as communist, anarchist and un-American," writes O'Leary. "Graphics regularly pictured Uncle Sam guiding American workmen away from the influence of swarthy agitators. The term *un-American* first came into significant usage as a political epithet during this period when 'true Americans' used it against striking immigrant workers and later against any militant opponents of the economic order, immigrant or native-born."[1]

In 1886, during a time of substantial labor unrest, Theodore Roosevelt, himself a rich employer, talked of setting worker against worker in the name of patriotism: "My men are hard-working laboring men, who work longer hours for no greater wages than most of the strikers; but they are *Americans through and through*. I believe nothing would give them greater pleasure than a chance with rifles at one of the mobs."[2] The Ford Motor Company sponsored Americanization programs for its employees: patriotism was equated with labor discipline and compliant worker attitudes. Other business firms fashioned programs modeled after Ford's.[3]

War often brings out the worst aspects of superpatriotism. In 1917, as the nation plunged into hostilities with Germany, domestic labor disputes were treated as acts of outright disloyalty. President Woodrow Wilson warned that the "masters of Germany" were using American liberals, socialists, and "the leaders of labor" to "carry out their designs."[4] Federal and state authorities suppressed radical publications, issued injunctions against strikes, harassed and jailed labor organizers, and launched legislative hearings, mass arrests, deportations, and political trials against labor militants. About a thousand people were sentenced to prison for denouncing the war as a "rich man's venture," some for as much as thirty years.[5]

In the 1930s, during the Great Depression, corporations like Ford took matters into their own hands, hiring mobsters and company thugs to beat union organizers and terrorize strikers.[6] Corporate-sponsored ultranationalist violence occurred in other capitalist countries as well. During the rise of fascism in Italy, Lithuania, Germany, Hungary, and Japan, "patriotic" goon squads were hired by business owners to smash labor unions and leftist political parties and publications.[7]

Sometimes the menace from within consisted of nothing more than an influx of poor and peaceful immigrants. For generations, successive waves of newcomers—with their different appearances and alien ways—were seen as undermining the American Way of Life. Those immigrants who manifested any political deviancy or labor militancy risked incarceration and deportation.[8]

More recently, in 2002, with the much hyped "war on terrorism" in full swing, the federal government ordered 82,000 immigrant men to register with federal enforcement agencies. The targeted group consisted almost entirely of persons from twenty-four Muslim countries. Not a single person caught in this dragnet was charged with a terrorist crime. Approximately 13,000 were indicted for overstaying their visas or for relatively minor violations, such as failure to report a change of address. Thousands were held incommunicado or summarily deported. Thousands more faced prolonged detention without a hearing or benefit of legal counsel.[9]

☆

Another alarming issue regularly magnified by the authorities and the media is the problem of crime. More than a half-century ago, Dwight Eisenhower campaigned his way into the White House on a platform that promised to fight "communism, crime, and corruption." In all the years that followed, political officeholders have heaped praise upon themselves for tirelessly waging a *war on crime* and a *war on drugs*, outdoing each other in trying to appear "tough" on this issue. Police and prison budgets skyrocketed, as did prison populations (the latter consisting heavily of nonviolent drug offenders serving draconian sentences). Under such bombardments, public apprehension about crime accelerated far more precipitously than the actual crime rate.

Today America is a nation feeling itself under siege from its criminal element. It is a land of gated communities, heavily guarded apartment towers, and millions of households armed with guns ready to dispatch unidentified trespassers. Fear of crime is supplemented with fear of ethnic minorities, terrorists, immigrants, foreigners, gays, feminists, rampaging teenagers, and outspoken peace protesters—in what amounts to a generalized *culture of fear*.

Menacing images are implanted in our brains during our most imaginative and malleable years. In the United

States, millions of children spend thousands of hours in front of the television set each year, ingesting a steady diet of violence-ridden programs. By the time the average teenager is graduated from high school he or she will have witnessed about 13,000 TV killings and many times that number of assaults, fistfights, robberies, shoot-outs, rapes, and attempted rapes. A survey by the National Institute of Mental Health found that the level of fear among children increases with heavy television viewing. Very young children, unable to grasp the motives behind the violence, tend to see almost everyone on TV as involved in a universal mode of brutality and threat.[10]

Not just children. Adults too ingest a steady diet of shows that feature every known violent act. Deranged murderers terrorize train passengers, kidnappers torment and kill their captives, terrorized women career about in their homes stalked by determined intruders, vampires slurp the blood of trembling maidens, ghoulish maniacs massacre people with chain saws, and so on. In 1992, in my book about the entertainment media, I wrote, "After enough days, months, and years of consuming this kind of fare, we might well be ready to vote for authoritarian law-and-order candidates, support the death penalty, increase military spending, bomb Iraq, buy a gun, and shoot anyone who strolls across our lawn after dusk."[11]

Numerous movies and television shows regularly glorify the rogue cop who operates outside the law in order to more effectively vanquish the evildoers. Ridden with fear, the public is not squeamish about tough law officers who throw away the rule book. If anything, many citizens cheer the police onward regardless of how brutally they might behave—whether in crime shows or in real life. People who live in fear of being harmed by perpetrators are not too concerned about individual rights and other constitutional niceties. The last thing they want is for police to "have their hands tied" in their war on crime.

☆

Children's adventure shows and video games also help propagate a culture of fear, and provide the dehumanizing practice of destroying human targets. One recently marketed electronic game designed for eight to thirteen-year-olds offers a "new race of powerful hybrid warriors" who contest alien invaders trying to take over the world.[12] A study of the most watched children cartoon shows reveals a pattern. Episodes tend to have one main evil leader who is accompanied by ferocious animals or by foreigners with unpleasant accents or other odd-looking characters who turn out to be sadistic scientists and assassins.[13]

In the thriller films pitched to older audiences, the basic paradigm is roughly the same: The world is swarming with fearsome aggressors who want to do us in. Virtuous Americans are menaced by evil foreigners, communists, cutthroats, diabolic geniuses, screaming savages, alien space invaders, giant asteroids, slimy serpentine creatures from beneath the lagoon, murderous mutant microbes, and other natural and supernatural perils. The ordinary people seem unable to defend themselves through collective action. Their role is to run hither and thither screaming to be saved from the menace. And saved they are—after suffering enough casualties—by individual heroes or state authorities who resort to generous applications of violence to make everything nice again. Good guys and their enemies never get together to negotiate a peaceful settlement. They only meet to go at each other's throats.[14]

Fed a lifelong diet of such offerings, many Americans have little difficulty accepting the picture painted by our leaders of a world full of vicious adversaries, lurking within and without our borders, just waiting to pounce upon us. These malefactors can only be deterred by more police, more prisons, more repressive laws at home, and a huge high-tech global military establishment to deal with the menace abroad.

Frightened people in want of protection do not desire rulers who are overly scrupulous about the methods they use. They prefer ones who are unfettered by the niceties of international law and justice. They want leaders who will stop at nothing when dealing with enemies who themselves purportedly will stop at nothing. They believe we need to fight fire with fire; we need to be ruthless and unsparing in order to prevent the evildoers from messing with us; we must maintain our credibility as a great power by demonstratinge our willingness to act forcefully anywhere in the world. Just as many Americans cheer the tough rogue cop who protects them from sinister perpetrators at home, so do they rally around the tough national leader who protects them from one or another perceived global menace.

☆

In early 2003, on the eve of the second war on Iraq, Americans reached new levels of superpatriotic panic when they turned their fear—and with it their hostility—toward the French. The *French*? France vetoed the US resolution calling for United Nations support of military action against Iraq. Other UN Security Council members such as Germany, Russia, and China also failed to support the US resolution. But it was the French who dared to play the lead opposition role during the debate.

US media pundits and right-wing talk show hosts lost no time in launching Francophobic attacks: How dare the French try to keep us from having our way against Iraq. Don't they remember how America rescued them in World Wars I and II? If it wasn't for us, they would be speaking German today. In any case, what is a second-rate nation like France doing with a permanent seat and veto on the UN Security Council? In his *New York Times* column, that tireless and tiresome apologist for US empire, Thomas Friedman, declared, "France is becoming our enemy" and "This French mischief" is misleading the European Union.[15] For Friedman, the war against Iraq was the "most important liberal, revolutionary US democracy-building project" in decades, "one of the noblest things this country has ever attempted abroad."[16] How could the French not see this? On Fox network's *Special Report*, columnist Morton Kondracke grumbled, "I think the French are perfidious." His fellow right-wing panelist, Fred Barnes, agreed, calling the French "untrustworthy."[17]

Among some of the more unraveled superpatriots there was talk about returning the Statue of Liberty to France and erecting a newly fashioned monument of our own. Numerous eateries, including the cafeteria in the US House of Representatives, sprang to our nation's defense by renaming french fries "freedom fries." In various parts of the USA, French restaurants reported a drop in patronage, and groceries and supermarkets noted a decline in the sale of French wines and cheeses. Some French cultural events in the USA, including films, art shows, and concerts, were subjected to boycotts and even threats from anonymous callers; some were canceled out of fear that something untoward might happen. Not surprisingly, the French ambassador to the United States, Jean-David Levitte, bemoaned the campaign of "denigration and lies" that seemed to overtake America.[18]

The hostility expressed toward the French was soon projected onto the French themselves. By criticizing US actions, they were in effect siding with our "enemies," thereby demonstrating their own enmity toward us. An American travel agent in Paris, interviewed on NPR, having scheduled a tour of France for some thirty Americans, reported that all but one had canceled their reservations. The one exception was a man who said he would make the trip only if given round-the-clock bodyguard protection. In 2003 many other would-be US tourists called off their trips to France, not wishing to subject themselves to the perils posed by the implacable Gauls. It should be noted that less fearful Americans visiting or residing in France reported no incidents of violence directed against them by angry French mobs. It seems the perfidious French had no idea that they were supposed to be preying upon American visitors.

At about that time, an acquaintance of mine, who works as a physician's assistant in Las Vegas and whose family has resided in the USA for generations, tells of a patient who noted her French-sounding name tag and asked in all seriousness, "Should I be worried?" Indeed, he should. He should be worried about why he is so easily manipulated by his rulers into entertaining wacko apprehensions.

1. O'Leary, *To Die For*, 61.
2. Quoted in Sender Garlin, *Three American Radicals* (Boulder, Colo: Westview, 1991), 115 (italics in the original).
3. O'Leary, *To Die For*, 238, 242.

4. O'Leary, *To Die For*, 227.

5. See William Preston Jr., *Aliens and Dissenters: Federal Suppression of Radicals, 1903–1933*, 2nd ed. (Urbana, Ill.: University of Illinois, 1994).

6. See Richard Boyer and Herbert Morais, *Labor's Untold Story*, 3rd ed. (New York: United Electrical, Radio and Machine Workers of America, 1972; and Thomas Reppetto, *American Mafia* (New York: Henry Holt, 2004.

7. Barrington Moore Jr., *Social Origins of Dictatorship and Democracy* (Boston: Beacon Press, 1966), 298.

8. Preston, *Aliens and Dissenters*, passim.

9. Report by Tammy Johnson, *ColorLines Magazine*, 2003.

10. David Pearl, *Television and Behavior* (Washington, D.C.: National Institute of Mental Health, 1982).

11. Michael Parenti, *Make-Believe Media: The Politics of Entertainment* (Belmont, Calif.: Wadsworth, 1992), 114.

12. Described in the *San Francisco Chronicle*, 14 December 2003.

13. See Petra Hesse and Ted Stimpson, "Images of the Enemy on Children's Television," *Propaganda Review*, summer 1989.

14. For a more extended discussion, see my *Make-Believe Media*, chapter 10.

15. *New York Times*, 18 September 2003.

16. *New York Times*, 30 November 2003.

17. Quoted in *New York Times*, 9 February 2003.

18. Stephen Sartarelli, "Where Did Our Love Go?" *Nation*, January 12–19. 2004.

11   ARE THE PLUTOCRATS PATRIOTIC?

OF THE PEOPLE WHO OCCUPY THE HIGHER circles of government and industry, most are from wealthy backgrounds. They and their loyal minions populate the boards of trustees of corporations, foundations, and institutions of higher learning. They own or otherwise have ready access to the giant media conglomerates. Some of them finance conservative think tanks. The more politically active among them move in and out of the top policy positions in Washington. Though relatively few in number, they own the lion's share of the nation's material resources. They set the interest rates and control the money supply. They play a dominant role in determining the wage levels and working conditions of millions. They enjoy oligarchic control of the major technologies of industrial production and communication. Taken together, these various elite groupings compose what might be called a *plutocracy*, a system of rule by and for the wealthy.

They do not operate with perfect cohesion. They sometimes have differences among themselves, and endure confusions and setbacks. Still, on the basic issues they hold to a common class interest, dedicated to seeing that the capital accumulation process continues unabated. Their wealth serves their power and their power serves their wealth.

Plutocratic rulers are among the major purveyors of superpatriotic enthusiasm but they rarely practice what they preach. They hail the idea of a "healthy America," yet they resist universal health-care programs, defund public health services, and work closely with the giant pharmaceutical and insurance industries to make health care highly profitable for a few corporations and painfully expensive for the rest of us.

They urge us on to ever greater feats of economic sacrifice and self-reliance, and tell us not to expect "government handouts," while they and their giant firms annually pocket hundreds of billions of dollars in government loan guarantees, bailouts, risk capital, equity capital, export subsidies, and enormously lucrative government contracts. They insist that everyone should shoulder the burdens of public debt and public expenditure, but they repeatedly push through tax cuts for their wealthy class.

In addition, they regularly enjoy billions in tax credits and tax write-offs, and often are outright tax evaders. The Internal Revenue Service estimates that offshore sub-sidiaries and tax havens cost the US Treasury $70 billion a year and billions more in unpaid state and local taxes.[1]

Superpatriotic plutocrats also manifest little interest in conserving America's environmental treasure. Instead, they allow timber and mining interests and agribusiness to plunder our natural terrain. They pursue fossil fuel and nuclear energy policies that wreak havoc on our land, waters, and atmosphere. They treat the natural resources of the country as so much disposable material for fast-buck profits. They say they love America even as they inflict gashing wounds upon its landscape.

☆

The ruling elites intone endlessly about family values, moral character, and clean living while themselves falling well short of these standards, being no more pristine than the rest of us in their personal lives and often seriously corrupt and dishonest in their public capacities—as the Enron, WorldCom, Halliburton, Harkin, and other multi-billion-dollar corporate scandals demonstrated. The cor-porate criminals used illicit accounting schemes and insider trading to filch billions of dollars from worker pension funds and small investors. The cost of low-level street crime in 2002 was $18 billion, while the cost of antitrust violations and other corporate crimes was $250 billion.[2] Such criminality does not fit well with the plutocracy's claim to civic virtue and patriotism.

It cannot be very patriotic to pilfer federal, state, and local treasuries and squander US tax dollars. Yet in the hands of our superpatriotic plutocrats, the federal surplus of $281 billion that existed in 2000 dissolved into a budget-busting deficit of $480 billion by fiscal year 2004, due mostly to huge subsidies and multibillion-dollar tax cuts to very rich individuals and corporations.

It is not very patriotic to routinely overcharge the US government for supplies and services, or submit falsely bloated noncompetitive bids for government contracts, or provide shoddy goods to US military personnel in combat zones. Yet in February 2004, the Pentagon opened a criminal fraud investigation of Halliburton, the giant Texas oil-services firm, for overcharging the US government at least $61 million for fuel transported into Iraq from Kuwait. US military commanders in Iraq told Pentagon chiefs that they lacked sanitary services and blast-proof barriers that a Halliburton subsidiary was supposed to provide. Halliburton was also being investigated for overcharging $16 million for meal services to the military and various other potentially scandalous dealings.[3]

It is not very patriotic to engage in war profiteering. In November 2003, a provision was inserted into the $87 billion spending bill slated for Iraq that would have made it a felony to overcharge the government for any goods or services intended for war or reconstruction in Iraq and

Afghanistan. But a Republican-controlled congressional conference committee deleted the provision from the final version of the bill.

It is not patriotic to fix prices in order to overcharge American consumers billions of dollars for goods and services. It is not patriotic to evade occupational safety standards, to force employees to work unpaid overtime, to violate the National Labor Relations Act by firing workers for their union organizing efforts. Yet these are all common plutocratic practices.

☆

The plutocrats profess a devotion to American democracy, yet through their state security agencies they repeatedly violate democratic practice and principle, resorting to harassment and suppression of dissident organizations, launching police attacks on street protesters, using planted evidence, false arrests, wiretapping, infiltration, and other dirty tricks against law-abiding citizens whose only crime has been to voice criticisms of plutocratic policies at home and abroad. The US Patriot Act allows federal agents to conduct surveillance and searches against any US citizen without having to show probable cause. The government now has broad access to everybody's business and personal records, including library and book-buying habits.[4]

The plutocrats have been subverting what is left of our democratic sovereignty in a series of "free trade" agreements with other capitalist nations. With such accords as

GATT, GATS, NAFTA, CAFTA, and FTAA, the private corporations of one country can enjoin the government of another country from implementing environmental regulations and consumer and worker safety standards if these are deemed to be "restraints on trade." The "free trade" agreements can prohibit federal, state, and local governments from providing not-for-profit human services when such services create "lost market opportunities" or in other ways "interfere" with the investments of foreign corporations that want to enter these markets.

The accords are designed to gut essential public services and protections. The superpatriots in the White House have imposed these agreements upon us with no consultation or approval by governors, state assemblies, or city councils, with virtually no public input, and in the face of opposition from the peoples of countries throughout the world, including the United States. What is being lost is not only the public services and regulations themselves but the *democratic sovereign right* of Americans (and peoples of other nations) to promote such protective laws and programs. The free-market right to invest is elevated above every other public right, including the right to self-governance. In effect, the international moneyed interests assume a veto power over most public policy and democratic legislation.[5]

The plutocrats tell us of their devotion to building a prosperous America for all. Yet many companies move their manufacturing beyond our borders to low-wage markets. In 2004, the White House released a report that officially endorsed this policy, saying in part, "When a good or service is produced more cheaply abroad, it makes more sense to import it than to make it or provide it domestically."[6] As a consequence of this outsourcing to cheap labor markets abroad, US manufactory employment lost 2.7 million jobs in 2001 to 2003 alone. By early 2004, with the economy showing signs of coming out of a long recession, job growth lagged so far behind that people spoke of a "jobless recovery."[7]

The goal of the transnational corporation is to become truly transnational, poised above the sovereign power of any particular nation, while being served by the sovereign powers of all nations. Cyril Siewert, chief financial officer of Colgate Palmolive Company, could have been speaking for all transnationals when he remarked, "The United States doesn't have an automatic call on our [corporation's] resources. There is no mindset that puts this country first."[8] Like any good plutocrat, Siewert puts his company first.

☆

The hypocritical quality of the plutocracy's patriotism is nowhere more blatantly displayed than in its dealings with the Nazi regime before and during World War II. After Adolph Hitler took state power in Germany in 1933, he set about establishing a repressive reactionary government that abolished labor unions, drastically reduced wages, eliminated worker benefits, ignored occupational safety standards, privatized various state enterprises, heavily subsidized big business, and drastically cut taxes for the very rich. Hitler also pursued an aggressive foreign policy that sent tremors across Europe. He annexed Austria, the Czech Sudetenland and eventually all of Czechoslovakia, and launched a massive arms buildup that augured a major war in Europe.

It was not long before numerous US corporate giants, including Du Pont, Ford, General Motors, Texaco, General Electric, Union Carbide, Westinghouse, Goodrich, Standard Oil of New Jersey, J. P. Morgan, IBM, and ITT were doing a booming business in the Third Reich, unable to resist the low wages, low business taxes, and high profits. Henry Ford, Irénée Du Pont, Tom Watson of IBM, Torkild Rieber of Texaco, and other plutocrats became great admirers of Hitler. "American corporations made a lot of money in Hitler's Germany; this, and not the Führer's alleged charisma, is the reason the owners and managers of these corporations adored him."[9] There were other reasons why they adored him. Some, like Henry Ford, openly shared Hitler's anti-Semitism, and all of them welcomed his anticommunism, seeing Hitler as a savior who would vanquish the Soviet Union and rescue Europe from Red revolution. If the acts of political terror and mass murder perpetrated by the Führer disturbed the US plutocrats, they gave little sign of it.

When Hitler launched his war of conquest in 1939, the US plutocrats willingly collaborated—and continued to do so even after Germany and the United States became belligerents in December 1941! Throughout occupied Europe, they made eager use of the slave labor provided by Nazi authorities. According to declassified documents from Dutch intelligence and US government archives, Prescott Bush, father and grandfather of the two Bush presidents, made lush profits off Auschwitz slave labor. His Union Banking Corporation helped Thyssen make the Nazi steel that killed Allied solders, and helped finance Thyssen's coal mines which regularly worked Jewish prisoners to death. The Bush family is heir to these Holocaust profits.[10]

US-owned factories in Nazi occupied Europe supplied the tanks, trucks, fighter planes, bombers, oil imports, synthetic fuels, synthetic rubber, and advanced communication systems that greatly enhanced the Nazis' capability to wage war. Without these crucial materials, it would have been impossible for German forces to kill American and other Allied troops, sink American ships, and bomb British cities. Likewise, IBM prospered in Germany and the occupied territories by supplying the technology needed to identify, enslave, and exterminate millions of European Jews and other victims.[11]

Throughout the war, US corporate chiefs were able to maintain direct ownership and control over their German subsidiaries with minimal interference from the Nazis, who were primarily interested in keeping war production going. US authorities did nothing to stop the big companies from servicing the Nazi war machine. President

Roosevelt even gave an order not to bomb US corporate properties in Germany and Nazi-occupied Europe. Thus, while the German city of Cologne was leveled, its Ford factory—providing armed vehicles used to kill American troops—was untouched; after a while it was used by German civilians as an air-raid shelter.[12]

There was much propaganda at home praising Big Business for building America's defenses and winning "the war of production." US leaders needed Corporate America's technology and oil resources as much as did the Nazis, so they looked the other way and did nothing about the cozy relationship between Hitler and US business. Trials and imprisonment would have made it difficult for the corporate collaborators to assist the US war effort, Charles Higham notes. Furthermore, the US government feared that a scandalous exposure would have damaged public morale, caused strikes, and perhaps incited mutiny in the military ranks. With the advent of the Cold War— which US leaders did so much to provoke—it was considered all the more imperative to disregard the Nazi collaborationist role played by Corporate America.[13]

The story gets worse. After the war, rather than being prosecuted for aiding and abetting the enemy, ITT collected $27 million from the US government for damages inflicted on its German plants by Allied bombings. And General Motors received over $33 million for damages. Ford and other companies collected considerable sums. Faced with class-action lawsuits in 1999–2000, growing numbers of corporations admitted having used and profited greatly from unpaid slave labor supplied from Nazi concentration camps.[14] But no US corporate manager has ever been prosecuted for complicity in these war crimes.

If this is patriotism, then what is treason?

1. Center for Corporate Policy newsletter, October 2003, Washington, D.C.; and Jonathan Blattmachr, "The Loophole Artist," *New York Times Magazine*, 21 December 2003.

2. Street crime costs are reported by the FBI; corporate crime costs are estimated by criminal justice scholar Francis Cullen, cited by M. M. Acosta in *San Francisco Chronicle*, 16 November 2003. The FBI refuses to keep statistics on corporate crime.

3. *USA Today*, 20 February 2004; *New York Times*, 24 February 2004; Associated Press, 11 March 2004.

4. Joseph A. Palermo, "Here We Go Again, Reliving History with the Patriot Act," *Because People Matter*, January/February 2004.

5. John R. MacArthur, *The Selling of "Free Trade": NAFTA, Washington and the Subversion of American Democracy* (New York: Hill and Wang, 2000); and Chris Slevin, "Bush Poised to Trade Away Sovereignty," *Public Citizen News*, May/June 2003.

6. Quoted in *Democratic News* (publication of Democratic National Committee), 13 February 2004.

7. Sam Zuckerman, "Feeble Growth in U.S. Jobs" *San Francisco Chronicle*, 7 February 2004; and the special report "Looking Offshore," *San Francisco Chronicle*, 7 March 2004.

8. Quoted in *New York Times*, 21 May 1989.

9. Jacques R. Pauwels, "Profits *Über Alles*! American Corporations and Hitler," *Labour/Le Travail*, 51, Spring 2003.

10. See Webster G. Tarpley and Anton Chaitkin, *George Bush: The Unauthorized Biography* (Washington, D.C.: Executive Intelligence Review, 1991); and John Loftus and Mark Aarons, *The Secret War Against the Jews: How Western Espionage Betrayed the Jewish People* (New York: St. Martin's Press, 1997).

11. Charles Higham, *Trading with the Enemy* (New York: Dell, 1983); Reinhold Billstein et al., *Working for the Enemy: Ford, General Motors, and Forced Labor during the Second World War* (New York: Berghahn, 2000); and Edwin Black, *IBM and the Holocaust* (London: Crown Publishers, 2001), 297–99.

12. Eyewitness report by E. F. Patterson, *Ramparts*, August 1974; and Pauwels,"Profits *Über Alles!*"

13. Higham, *Trading with the Enemy*, 12–15.

14. *New York Times*, 29 April 2000.

12 SUPPORT OUR TROOPS (CUT THEIR BENEFITS)

BEING THE SUPERPATRIOTS THEY ARE, THE plutocrats equate military service with true patriotism. But while they heap praise upon those who "serve our country," they themselves rarely join up. The men and women who enlist into the military come disproportionately from blue-collar and lower-middle-class families. They are often young people who have trouble finding a job or cannot afford a higher education. Graduates of Yale, Harvard, and Princeton rarely sign up for the Marines. They head for law school or Wall Street or the family business or their favorite avocation. As prime examples, consider the *chickenhawks*, a label applied to those privileged leaders who are virulently hawkish on war but strenuously evasive of military service.

Topping the chickenhawk list is President George W. Bush. In his youth, he won entry into Yale University more on pedigree than performance. Later on, seeking to evade the draft, he got himself admitted to the Texas Air National Guard despite his low score on the pilot aptitude test. As he explained it without a hint of apology, "I was not prepared to shoot my eardrum out with a shotgun in order to get a deferment. Nor was I willing to go to Canada. So I chose to better myself by learning how to fly airplanes."[1]

Bush was accepted into the Guard ahead of hundreds of other applicants who were waiting to join in order to escape duty in Vietnam. His unit, the 147th Fighter Group, was nicknamed the "Champagne Unit" because it had so many sons of Texas privilege. How he jumped to the head of the line is itself a story. A rich Houston businessman and longtime friend of the Bush family approached Ben Barnes, then Speaker of the Texas House, and asked him to help George W. gain entry into the Guard. Only when questioned under oath did Barnes admit that he had spoken to the Texas Air National Guard on Bush's behalf.[2]

Bush's payroll records show that he failed to report for duty for eight months between May 1972 and May 1973. He failed to take a required flight physical examination in 1972, and was suspended from flying, an action that should have set off an inquiry but did not. In February 2004, the White House released documents that purportedly proved that Bush had shown up for duty in 1972 with the 187th Fighter Group in Alabama (to which he had transferred in order to work on a political campaign). But White House officials could not say what duties he performed (nor could Bush), and no one in the 187th came forward with recollections of having served with him. His commanders say he did not appear for duty at bases in Texas and Alabama where he had been assigned during that 1972–1973 period.[3]

Instead of being prosecuted for desertion, Bush was awarded an honorable discharge eight months early in order to attend Harvard Business School. Bush's military records should have contained paperwork explaining why he was allowed to leave well before his enlistment ended, but no explanation has been released. It seems this presidential superpatriot received favorable treatment to get into the National Guard and favorable treatment to get out.

Then there is Vice President Dick Cheney, who explained why he did not serve during the Vietnam War: "I had other priorities in the '60s than military service." Cheney received draft deferments as a college student. Upon graduating he was able to avoid the draft by getting married. But in 1964, the government announced married men would be drafted, unless they were fathers. Nine months and two days after that announcement, in an act of superb timing, the Cheneys had their firstborn.

Other high-ranking superpatriotic members of the Bush administration who avoided the draft included Karl Rove,

Richard Perle, Paul Wolfowitz, John Ashcroft, Elliott Abrams John Bolton, Douglas Feith, and Andrew Card; so too Republican congressional leaders Trent Lott, Dennis Hastert, Dick Armey and Tom DeLay; and we must not forget right-wing media hawks like George Will, William Kristol, and Rush Limbaugh.[4] DeLay reportedly said that he would have served but all the draft slots in his area were taken up by blacks. And rabid radio reactionary Limbaugh got a medical deferment because of his "anal cysts"—a condition that normally responds to treatment but in Limbaugh's case proved oddly incurable for the duration of the Vietnam War.

One is not required to have served in the military in order to formulate governmental policy. Indeed, the principle of civilian rule over the military is enshrined in our Constitution. What is so objectionable about the superpatriotic chickenhawks is not their lack of combat experience as such; it is the hypocritical disparity between their tough jingoistic war stance and their own active avoidance of the draft. They pursue wars with all their hearts and minds but not with their bodies. They escaped conscription by using draft deferments, dubious medical exemptions, and family influence.

Years after Vietnam, now occupying prominent public positions, these same chickenhawks again brayed for blood, this time targeting Iraq. Once again they were ready to send other families' offspring into the fray, not their own. They equated militarism with patriotism and preached sacrifice and devotion to flag and country. Yet their own patriotic sacrifices consisted mostly of sticking tiny American-flag pins into the lapels of their high-priced suits.

☆

If patriotism means supporting our troops, then no one is more lacking in patriotism than the ruling plutocracy. In 2003–2004, hundreds of US troops who had been wounded in Iraq were warehoused for months at places like Fort Stewart, Georgia, in hot, dirty, overcrowded cement barracks waiting for medical treatment. They had to hobble across the sand to use the bathroom, and had to pay for their toilet paper. And only after protests from the US Senate did the White House stop charging wounded soldiers $8.10 per day for their hospital meals.[5]

Many of the badly wounded said that they were seeing their pay and health benefits severely reduced now that they were no longer fit for active duty. More than 200,000 veterans of earlier wars have had to wait six months or longer for their first appointment with the Veterans' Administration. Thousands have waited years to get into overcrowded and understaffed VA hospitals to receive disability assistance, often being unable to pay their own living expenses in civilian life.[6] Not surprisingly, a large portion of the homeless are veterans of past wars, some with untreated mental and physical ailments.

In February 2002, at the very time he was sending thousands of troops to fight in Afghanistan, Bush junior proposed tripling the cost of medications to needy veterans. In 2003 his administration announced it was cutting off access to its health-care system for approximately 164,000 veterans, and slicing out $1.5 billion in military housing and medical facility funding. Also in 2003, while heaping praise on the men and women doing military service, Bush refused a congressional request for a relatively modest $275 million to cover veterans' health-care needs. In his 2004 budget, he slashed $2 billion from the VA's already insufficient funds. The Bush administration even ordered officials to stop publicizing health benefits available to veterans. While praising the National Guard and Reservists for serving in Iraq, Bush opposed a proposal to allow them access to the Pentagon's health insurance system. His administration also announced its plan to reduce monthly imminent-danger pay (from $225 to $150) and family-separation allowance (from $250 to $100) for troops getting shot at in combat zones.[7]

There are other strange ways that the plutocracy supports our troops. For experimental purposes, the government has repeatedly exposed US military personnel to dangerously toxic substances. From 1962 to 1973, the Pentagon used potentially harmful chemical and biological agents in fifty secret tests involving thousands of unwitting US troops, a fact that was not publicized until 2002.[8] In addition, thousands of "GI guinea pigs" were subjected to atomic bomb tests after World War II, tens of thousands were exposed to Agent Orange during the

Vietnam War, and many more were contaminated by depleted uranium (DU) during the Gulf War of 1991. The Pentagon never warned their own troops about DU, and for years officials denied that a problem existed. Over 183,000 Gulf veterans filed for disability, complaining of aching joints, memory problems, nausea, and illness. Almost 10,000 have died prematurely. Many family members also have sickened, and a disproportionate number of Gulf veteran offspring suffer from birth defects.

Populations in Indochina, Yugoslavia, Iraq, Colombia, and elsewhere that have been exposed to DU or Agent Orange or other toxic sprays have suffered in far greater numbers than have US service personnel and their families, but these foreigners do not even enter the superpatriotism equation except as defenseless targets.

☆

One of the things plutocrats like about war is its huge financial cost. The more taxpayers' money spent on war contracts, the more plentiful are the profits. Many supplies and services, including those relating to food and housing, traditionally performed by soldiers, have been handed over to private contractors such as Kellogg Brown and Root, a Halliburton subsidiary. The result is that US troops in Iraq endured months of poor living conditions, inedible food, and low-performing equipment. Some of the private contractors even failed to show up because of the dangers presented by the Iraqi armed resistance.[9]

In 2003, a report by the Congressional Budget Office revealed that only about $2.5 billion of the $4 billion expended monthly on the Iraq War could be accounted for by the White House and the Pentagon! Meanwhile, the Pentagon barred French, German, and Russian companies from competing for the multibillion-dollar contracts for the reconstruction of Iraq. All the reconstruction and oil extraction business was given to Halliburton, Bechtel, and some seventy other US firms, usually at noncompetitive fees set by the companies themselves.[10]

In 2003 the Bush administration sought to block a group of American veterans—who had been tortured in Iraqi prisons during the Gulf War of 1991—from collecting any of the hundreds of millions of dollars in frozen Iraqi assets that a federal court had awarded them. Administration lawyers argued that the frozen assets would be better spent on Iraqi reconstruction contracts. "No amount of money can truly compensate these brave men and women for the suffering they went through," said a White House spokesman.[11] And so, no amount of money was allocated to them.

As American casualties mounted in Iraq, President Bush turned a cold shoulder to the grieving families of the slain servicemen and women. For the first time in US history, dead Americans were brought home in secrecy. Bush would not attend military funerals or memorials as previous presidents had done. The Pentagon notified all news media that no television and photographic coverage was allowed of coffins returning to Dover Air Force Base. The military brass explained that this was to "respect the privacy of the families." Actually, with no pictures of flag-draped caskets, the public was less likely to think of them. Even the term "body bags" was no longer used. The spin artists at the Pentagon now referred to the plastic encasements that carried slain soldiers as "transfer tubes."[12]

☆

So we return to the question posed in the previous chapter: are our plutocratic rulers patriotic? Well, yes, they are, but only when it serves their purposes and only when it does not cost them anything. They are patriotic in that hollow abstract way, a patriotism empty of content, a patriotism of showy flurries and words, words, words. They may love their country but not the people in it, not the taxpayers, not the voters, and certainly not the poor souls who are sent off to fight their wars.

[1]. Quoted in *Nation*, 14 November 2003

[2]. *New York Times*, 15 February 2004.

[3]. *Los Angeles Times*, 11 February 2004; *Boston Globe*, 10 February 2004; *New York Times*, 13 February 2004; also on Bush's early career, see Joe Conason, *Big Lies* (Thomas Dunne/St. Martin's, 2003). For a complete listing of chickenhawks in the Bush administration, see www.nhgazette.com/chickenhawks.html.

4. Tim Harper, "Pentagon Keeps Dead Out of Sight," *Toronto Star*, 5 November 2003.

5. *Washington Post*, 17 January 2003; UPI, 17 October 2003; CBS News, 18 January 2003; CNN Report, 17 July 2003;

6. *San Francisco Chronicle*, 12 May 2003; Gannett News Service, 23 October 2003; *Washington Post*, 17 January 2003; *Army Times*, 30 June 2003.

7. *New York Times*, 9 October 2002; and Associated Press, 1 July 2003.

8. *New York Times*, 11 August 2003.

9. Associated Press, 19 September 2003, and *New York Times*, 10 December 2003.

10. *New York Times*, 10 November 2003.

11. Tim Harper, "Pentagon Keeps Dead Out of Sight," *Toronto Star*, 5 November 2003; *New York Times*, 9 November 2003.

13   RULERS OF THE PLANET

US LEADERS HAVE LONG PROFESSED A DEDI-
cation to democracy, yet over the last half century they
have devoted themselves to overthrowing democratic governments in Guatemala, Guyana, the Dominican Republic,
Brazil, Chile, Uruguay, Syria, Indonesia (under Sukarno),
Greece (twice), Argentina (twice), Haiti (twice), Bolivia,
Jamaica, Yugoslavia, and other countries. These governments were all guilty of pursuing policies that occasionally favored the poorer elements and infringed upon the
more affluent. In most instances, the US-sponsored coups
were accompanied by widespread killings of democratic
activists.[1]

US leaders have supported covert actions, sanctions, or
proxy mercenary wars against revolutionary governments

in Cuba, Angola, Mozambique, Ethiopia, Iraq (with the CIA ushering in Saddam Hussein's reign of repression), Portugal, South Yemen, Nicaragua, Cambodia, East Timor, Western Sahara, and elsewhere.

US interventions and destabilization campaigns have been directed against other populist nationalist governments, including Egypt, Lebanon, Peru, Iran, Syria, Zaire, Venezuela, the Fiji Islands, and Afghanistan (*before* the Soviets ever went into the country).

And since World War II, direct US military invasions or aerial attacks or both have been perpetrated against Vietnam, Laos, Cambodia, Cuba, the Dominican Republic, North Korea, Yugoslavia, Lebanon, Grenada, Panama, Libya, Somalia, and Iraq (twice).[2] There is no "rogue state," "axis of evil," or communist country that has a comparable record of such criminal aggression against other nations.

Be it a social democratic coalition government as with Allende in Chile or Arbenz in Guatemala, a populist nationalist one like Iran under Mossadegh, a Marxist-Leninist government as in Cuba and Vietnam, even a right-wing nationalist government as Iraq under Saddam Hussein—all had one thing in common, a desire to reclaim some portion of the land, natural resources, capital, labor, and markets that had been preempted by local plutocrats and giant foreign corporations.[3]

In contrast, US leaders have been markedly supportive of dictatorial capitalist client-states like Chile (under Pinochet), the Philippines (under Marcos), Iran (under the Shah), Zaire (under Mobutu), Peru (under Fujimoro), apartheid South Africa, autocratic Turkey, feudal Saudi Arabia and feudal Kuwait, and other autocracies like Turkey, Pakistan, and Nigeria. In short, Washington policymakers are less critical of democracy's real enemies than of capitalism's democratic opponents.

☆

US intervention in Africa is a story in itself. Through the World Bank and the IMF, US leaders have demolished African economies, including their public health and education sectors. Most African nations have sunk into a debt structure that leaves them in peonage to Western investors. US leaders also have fueled eleven wars on the continent, resulting in the death of more than 4 million people, with millions more facing malnutrition, starvation, and deepening poverty. Washington has given arms and military training to fifty African countries (out of a total of fifty-three), helping Africa to become the most war-torn region in the world. During the 1990s alone, thirty-two African countries experienced violent conflict.[4]

All this well-fueled strife has enabled the United States and other Western interests to attain control of Africa's abundant resources. The more war-ravaged and poverty-stricken are the African nations, the more ready they are to sell their labor and natural resources at rock-bottom prices. Asad Ismi reminds us that almost 80 percent of the strategic minerals that the USA requires are extracted from

Africa, including cobalt, platinum, gold, chromium, manganese, and uranium, ingredients needed to make jet engines, automotive vehicles, missiles, electronic components, iron, and steel.[5]

Africa also accounts for 18 percent of US oil imports (as compared to 25 percent from the Middle East), with new reserves yet to be tapped. The African continent in toto has been designated a vital interest area to the United States. Plans are in progress to build new US naval and military bases on the continent. And according to the African Oil Policy Initiative Group (composed of representatives from the Bush administration, the oil industry, Congress, and some foreign consultants), Washington intends to establish a regional military command structure in Africa "which could produce significant dividends in the protection of US investments."[6]

Not just in Africa but across the entire world, US policymakers have militarized nation after nation to fuel the military capacities of cooperative capitalist nations. In 2004, worldwide arms sales by the United States to other countries was about $40 billion, much of it going to nations like Saudi Arabia that do not even remotely maintain a democratic facade. Since World War II the US government has given some $240 billion in military aid to train, equip, and subsidize some 2.3 million troops and internal-security forces in more than eighty countries, not to defend these nations from outside invasion—since few have ever been threatened by attack from neighboring countries—but to protect ruling oligarchs and multinational corporate investors from the dangers of domestic insurgency.

How can we determine the purpose of this military aid? By observing that: (a) US-supported military and security forces and death squads in these various countries have been used repeatedly to destroy popular reformist movements and insurgencies within their own borders that advocate some kind of egalitarian redistributive politics. (b) US-sponsored forces have never been used to assist a popular reformist, let alone revolutionary, movement in any of these nations. (c) The regimes most likely to win US favor are those that are integrated into the global system of neoliberal corporate domination, that leave their economies open to foreign penetration on terms that are singularly favorable to transnational investors. (d) The regimes that are targeted as anti-West or anti-American are most likely to be committing the sin of egalitarian reform and national self-definition. And when there are no longer any leftist reformist governments to compete against, US globalists begin competing against other capitalist powers.

☆

US leaders have long struck a defensive pose: America is besieged by menacing opponents; we have no choice but to maintain this enormous military apparatus. In reality, far from having their backs to the wall, US policymakers have been pursuing total world domination. This policy has been explicitly enunciated by a right-wing think tank called Project for the New American Century (PNAC). A lengthy report of September 2000 titled *Rebuilding America's Defenses* lays out PNAC's vision for US global control, including a huge boost in military spending, an unwillingness to be bound by the restraints of international law, and a dramatic expansion of a US military presence and use of force around the world.[7]

Not only did the PNAC report serve as a blueprint for the Bush administration, but many of PNAC's members became White House policymakers, including Vice President Dick Cheney, Secretary of Defense Donald Rumsfeld, Deputy Secretary of Defense Paul Wolfowitz, and Undersecretary of State John Bolton. Numerous other PNAC members came to occupy important posts in the Bush administration, mostly in the Defense and State Departments.[8]

The goal of the PNAC plan is to take full advantage of America's unparalleled ability to maintain the United States "as the world's preeminent power." The intent is anything but defensive. Every means of coercion and domination is to be assiduously pursued. *Rebuilding America's Defenses* even hints that the United States might develop biological weapons "that can target specific genotypes" in order to "transform biological warfare from the realm of terror to a politically useful tool." "The goal," concludes Gregory Elich, "is nothing less than to expose the entire globe to the threat of US aggression while depriving relatively well-armed nations of the means of defense. . . ."[9]

The PNAC report bemoaned the fact that US public opinion might not go along with a totalistic global policy unless it felt compelled to do so in response to "some catastrophic and catalyzing event—like a new Pearl Harbor." In another of those seemingly fortuitous happenings that work so well for the plutocracy, the 11 September 2001 attacks on the World Trade Center and the Pentagon served as just such a catastrophic catalyst.

The role played by the Bush administration before and during 9/11 is still a subject of some controversy. The White House ignored repeated warnings proffered by the intelligence agencies of eleven other nations regarding an impending attack. Two senior Israeli intelligence experts journeyed to Washington a month before the attacks to alert the CIA and FBI to cells of terrorists said to be planning a big operation. The list they provided contained the names of four of the 9/11 hijackers, but none of them was arrested. A month before the attacks, one FBI agent wrote about a plan afoot to crash into the Twin Towers; that report was ignored.[10]

In the year before 9/11—as legally required—the US military launched fighter planes on at least sixty-seven occasions to chase suspicious aircraft or airliners that had moved significantly off their flight plan. But on 11 September itself, in the almost two hours during which the four airliners were hijacked and the attacks occurred, not a single US fighter plane took flight.

President Bush's own behavior suggests cover-up. First, he unsuccessfully opposed the formation of an independent bipartisan commission to investigate the events around 9/11. Then he tried to appoint former Secretary of State Henry Kissinger to head the investigation, a man whose entire career had been devoted to dissembling and misleading the public. Then Bush refused to hand over numerous documents requested by the commission. Meanwhile, US national security adviser Condeleeza Rice initially refused to testify and Bush backed her refusal, only changing his mind after much public pressure. And finally, he and Vice President Cheney refused to testify under oath, agreeing only to appear together at an off-the-record meeting. What did they have to hide?

☆

The administration's recalcitrance made no sense until it is set against the PNAC plan with its explicit longing for "a new Pearl Harbor." The PNAC populated White House seems to have done nothing to prevent the attacks despite any number of warnings. The disaster of 11 September 2001 served them well. Like another Pearl Harbor indeed, it mobilized public opinion behind US global objectives. After 9/11, and in keeping with the PNAC plan, Bush took a number of momentous steps.

First, he announced a "war on terrorism," inviting all the nations and organizations of the world to get in lock-step behind his administration, declaring: "Either you are with us or you are with the terrorists." Henceforth all other countries were to be categorized as either *coopera-*

tive (accepting US hegemony) or *adversarial* (not letting US leaders have their way in all things). Any recalcitrant nation ran the risk of being targeted for US attack.

Second, the White House declared that it would not be bound by any previous treaties or accords. International law was now nothing but an irksome restraint that the world's only superpower would brush aside whenever it wanted.

Third, Bush announced the US withdrawal from the Anti-Ballistic Missile Treaty. The nuclear arms race was to resume, and the USA would win it handily by establishing total domination of land, air, sea, and outer space.

Fourth, Bush removed the US signature from the treaty establishing the International Criminal Court. The court was a wonderful step taken by many nations to prosecute leaders and operatives of any nation who violated the human rights of others. Instead, US leaders pressured various countries to grant immunity from prosecution for all US governmental and military personnel.

Fifth, the White House announced its right to wage preemptive war against any nation it disliked. Various countries were fingered as being on Uncle Sam's hit list— some of the same ones as listed in the PNAC plan: Iraq, Iran, North Korea, and Syria for starters.

Sixth, war was pursued in Afghanistan, and major military bases were established in several other Central Asian states.

Seventh, a war of conquest was launched against Iraq. The PNAC plan, published a full year before the September 2001 attacks, shows that the Bush administration had intended to take military control of the Gulf region whether or not Saddam Hussein was still in power.

Eighth, the White House embarked upon a massive escalation in military spending, with $176 billion allocated in just the first six months of the war against Iraq. Given the enormous deficit that resulted from this kind of spending and tax breaks, Republicans called for cuts in the domestic budget, specifically such frivolous luxuries as health care for the elderly, disability assistance, environmental regulations and protections, old-age pensions, and public education. So the Empire feeds off the Republic.

The PNAC plan envisions a strategic confrontation with China, and a still greater permanent military presence in every corner of the world. The objective is not just power for its own sake but power to control the world's natural resources and markets, power to privatize and deregulate the economies of every nation in the world, and power to hoist upon the backs of peoples everywhere—including North America—the blessings of an untrammeled global "free market." The end goal is to ensure not merely the supremacy of global capitalism as such, but the supremacy of *American* global capitalism by preventing the emergence of any other potentially competing superpower or, for that matter, any potential regional power such as Iraq.

☆

In chapter seven I noted that US superpatriots believe their nation is possessed of matchless virtues that no other nation can claim. The United States supposedly has a special mission to fight tyranny, uplift less fortunate nations, and create a better world—even if that entails killing large numbers of anti-American infidels abroad. But the truth is US leaders are not dedicated to advancing social justice and democracy in the world. Their real dedication—as they sometimes will say—is to create a US-dominated free-market globalism. Such a patriotism is better recognized by its real name: imperialism.

1. On Afghanistan, see the discussion in my *The Terrorism Trap: September 11 and Beyond* (San Francisco: City Lights, 2002), chapter 4.

2. See the sources in previous note.

3. For evidence of these various cases, see my *Against Empire*; and the writings of James Petras, Gregory Elich, William Blum, Edward Herman, and Chalmers Johnson.

4. Asad Ismi, "Ravaging Africa," *Briarpatch*, February 2003.

5. Ismi, "Ravaging Africa."

6. Dena Montague, "Africa: The New Oil and Military Frontier," *Peacework*, October 2002; also Ismi, "Ravaging Africa."

7. Gregory Elich, "Imperial Enterprise: War Mongers Run Amuck," *Swans*, 17 March 2003, www.swans.com.

8. Other PNAC members in top positions in the Bush administration: Richard Perle, Eliot Cohen, Devon Cross, Stephen

Cambone, Richard Armitage, Lewis Libby, Don Zakheim, and William Kristol.

9. Elich, "Imperial Enterprise."
10. Michael Meacher in *Guardian* (UK), 6 September 2003; also *Daily Telegraph* (UK), 16 September 2001; and *Newsweek*, 20 May 2002.

14   "WHY DO THEY HATE US?"

WE CRITICS OF US FOREIGN POLICY HAVE argued that the best road to national safety and security lies neither in police state repression at home nor military conquests abroad but in a foreign policy that stops making the United States an object of hatred among people throughout the world.

Terrorism is a vicious form of political action directed against innocent and defenseless people, as the March 2004 massacre of train commuters in Madrid again demonstrated. Along with denouncing such attacks, we have to try to comprehend why they keep happening. The 11 September 2001 terrorist attacks on the World Trade Center and the Pentagon raised the question among many US commentators and citizens: "Why do they hate us?"

How could anyone want to do such a thing to the United States and us nice Americans? A number of the right-wing pundits who overpopulate the corporate media maintain that the "Islamic terrorists" attack us because we are prosperous, free, democratic, and secular; they want to change our ways. As CBS-TV anchorman Dan Rather remarked, "We are winners and they are losers, and that's why they hate us."

In fact, if we bother to listen to what the terrorists themselves actually say, they hate us not because of who we *are* but because of what we *do*—to them and their region of the world. The individuals who bombed the World Trade Center the first time, in 1993, sent a letter to the *New York Times* declaring that the attack was "in response for the American political, economic, and military support to Israel . . . and the rest of the dictator countries in the [Middle East] region."[1]

In November 2001, in his first interview after 9/11, Osama bin Laden had this to say: "This is a defensive Jihad. We want to defend our people and the territory we control. This is why I said that if we do not get security, the Americans will not be secure either." A year later, a taped message from Osama bin Laden began: "The road to safety [for America] begins by ending [US] aggression. Reciprocal treatment is part of justice. The [terrorist] incidents that have taken place . . . are only reactions and reciprocal actions."[2]

As early as 1989, former president Jimmy Carter told

the *New York Times*: "You only have to go to Lebanon, to Syria or to Jordan to witness first-hand the intense hatred among many people for the United States because we bombed and shelled and unmercifully killed totally innocent villagers—women and children and farmers and housewives—in those villages around Beirut. As a result of that . . . we became kind of a Satan in the minds of those who are deeply resentful. That is what . . . has precipitated some of the terrorists attacks."[3]

The Iraqi resistance to the US occupation (during 2003–2004) did not seem impelled by a hate-ridden envy of the United States as such but by a desire to get the Americans out of Iraq. The Iraqis resented the USA not because it was so free, prosperous, and secular but because US forces had delivered death and destitution upon their shattered nation. As exclaimed one Iraqi woman, whose relatives were killed by US troops, "God curse the Americans. God curse those who brought them to us."[4] Under the US occupation, unemployment had climbed to 50 percent, and villages and towns went without electricity, water, and sewage disposal for many months. Meanwhile, US companies were pumping out Iraqi oil, and privatizing and expropriating the country's entire economy.

An in-depth, five-year study of religiously motivated terrorism was conducted by Jessica Stern, who interviewed religious militants of all stripes. She found men and women who were propelled neither by hatred of US prosperity and democracy nor by nihilistic violence. Rather, they held a deep faith in the justice of their cause and in the possibility of transforming the world through violent sacrificial action.[5] The United States was not envied but resented for the repression and poverty its policies had imposed upon their countries.

☆

The bombings and invasions inflicted by US rulers upon the peoples of other nations are all for their own good, our rulers would have us think. Why the targeted populations cannot see this remains a mystery to the sponsors of Washington's "humanitarian wars." When asked why he thought some countries had a "vitriolic hatred for America," George W. Bush offered his superpatriotic mystification: "I'm amazed that there's such misunderstanding of what our country is about that people would hate us. Like most Americans, I just can't believe it because I know how good we are."[6]

But even the Pentagon allowed that what US leaders do abroad might have something to do with inciting terrorism. A 1997 Defense Department study concludes: "Historical data show a strong correlation between US involvement in international situations and an increase in terrorist attacks against the United States."[7] Such "US involvement," it should be noted, often consists of a state-sponsored terrorism that attacks popular movements throughout the world, killing labor leaders and workers,

peasants, students, journalists, clergy, teachers, and anyone else who supports a more egalitarian social order
within their own country.

People throughout the world are fearful of a US military
empire, with an unanswerable destructive capacity never
before seen in human history. This global force consists of
about half a million troops stationed at over 395 major
bases and hundreds of minor installations in some 120
nations, with large-scale deployment in 25 countries;
8,000 strategic nuclear weapons and 22,000 tactical ones;
and a navy greater in total tonnage and firepower than all
the other navies of the world combined, consisting of missile cruisers, nuclear submarines, nuclear aircraft carriers,
and destroyers that patrol every ocean.

US bomber squadrons and long-range missiles can
reach any target, delivering enough explosive force to
mangle the infrastructures of entire countries—as
demonstrated against Iraq in 1990–1991 and Yugoslavia
in 1999. US satellites and spy planes survey the entire
planet. In addition, the United States is developing a
capacity to conduct war from outer space. With only 5
percent of the earth's population, the United States
expends more military funds than all the other major
powers combined.[8]

Whole societies have been undermined and shattered
not only by US bombings and invasions but by US sanctions and monetary policies that have imposed a debt
peonage and poverty upon struggling nations. US-spon-

sored terrorism—in the form of death squads, paramilitaries, US-supported invasions, and occupations—has taken millions of lives in scores of other countries. Maybe all this has something to do with why they hate us.

1. *New York Times*, 9 January 1998. This and the next two citations were kindly provided to me by William Blum.
2. *Los Angeles Times*, 13 November 2002.
3. *New York Times*, 26 March 1989.
4. *San Francisco Chronicle*, 11 January 2004.
5. Jessica Stern, *Terror in the Name of God* (New York: Ecco, 2003).
6. *Boston Globe*, 12 October 2001.
7. US Department of Defense, Defense Science Board 1997 Summer Study Task Force on DOD Responses to Transnational Threats, October 1997, Final Report, vol. 1. HYPERLINK http://www.acq.osd.mil/dsb/trans.pdf, cited in William Blum, "Myth and Denial in the War Against Terrorism" forthcoming article.
8. On US military spending, see *Defense Monitor* November/December 2003, publication of the Center for Defense Information, Washington, D.C. On the US military empire, see the collection of articles in Carl Boggs, ed., *Masters of War: Militarism and Blowback in the Era of American Empire* (New York/London: Routledge, 2003).

15   REAL PATRIOTISM

IN CONTRAST TO THE SUPERPATRIOTS, there are the real patriots who care enough about their country to want to improve it. Their patriotism has a social content. They know that democracy is not just the ability to hold elections. Democracy must also serve the needs and interests of the *demos*, the people. Real patriots educate themselves about the real history of their country and are not satisfied with the flag-waving promotional fluff that passes for history. They find different things in our past to be proud of than do superpatriots, such as the struggle for enfranchisement, the abolitionist movement, the peace movement, the elimination of child labor, and the struggle for collective bargaining, the eight-hour day, occupational safety, and racial justice and gender equality.

In the real patriot's pantheon can be found Tom Paine, Harriet Tubman, Frederick Douglass, Mark Twain, Susan B. Anthony, Mother Jones, Big Bill Haywood, John Reed, Eugene Victor Debs, Elizabeth Gurly Flynn, Jeanette Rankin, Rosa Parks, Paul Robeson, A. J. Muste, Harry Bridges, Walter Reuther, Martin Luther King—and the millions in the ranks who championed social justice.

Real patriots do not easily succumb to popular fears about external menaces that are propagated by the plutocracy. Instead, they note the things that people really *should* fear: the potentially catastrophic threat of global warming, the baneful and overpowering influence of money in our political life; the growing instances of electoral coercion, fraud, and thievery; the overweening and unaccountable power of corporations; the rampant corporate crime that plunders billions of dollars from the public treasury and private savings; the underfunding and deterioration of public services; the gargantuan profit-driven military budget; the runaway national debt that siphons hundreds of billions from the public treasury each year and threatens the entire financial structure of the nation; the repressive laws that steal away our liberties under the guise of homeland security; and the oil-driven foreign policy of perpetual war and unlawful aggression that has made the United States the most feared and hated nation in the world.

While running for the Democratic presidential nomination, Senator John Edwards (D-N.C.) spoke about the "two Americas" we have today:

One America that does the work, another America that reaps the reward. One America that pays the taxes, another America that gets the tax breaks. One America that will do anything to leave its children a better life, another America that never has to do a thing because its children are already set for life. One America—middle-class America—whose needs Washington has long forgotten, another America—narrow-interest America—whose very wish is Washington's command. One America that is struggling to get by, another America that can buy anything it wants, even Congress and a president.

Real patriots ally themselves with that first America Edwards describes. They struggle for fundamental social change. They want to tax the rich, not low-income working people. They want to develop renewable nonpolluting wind, tidal, and solar energy sources, and swift safe mass transit systems with less reliance on toxic fossil fuels. In contrast to the profit-oriented conservative superpatriots who repeatedly profess their love for America but seem unconcerned about America's forests, rivers, wildlife, wetlands, water supplies, and overall ecological health, the real patriot puts environmental concerns before everything else, for without a livable ecology nothing else will survive.

☆

Real patriots advocate a freedom of speech and freedom of ideas in the major media that would include dissident Left views as well as the usual right-wing and conventional opinions we are constantly exposed to. Real patriots want some relief from the evasive, fatuous, mealymouthed, know-it-all empire-boosting pundits and conservative or otherwise insipid commentators. They want major media debates on the basic assumptions behind US foreign policy and free-market globalism. They want to reclaim the nation's airwaves, which belong not to the network bosses but to the people of the United States.

Some real patriots want a government that will go directly into not-for-profit production. They want a fair chance given to worker-controlled enterprises and public ownership. If private industry cannot provide for the needs of the people, cannot build homes and hospitals enough for all, then the public sector should do so—not by contracting it out to private profiteers but by direct production as during the New Deal when public workers made tents, cots, and shoes, and canned foods for the destitute—a not-for-profit production that created jobs, served human needs, and expanded individual spending power and the tax base, all done without the parasitic private investors making a penny on it.

Real patriots want to open up our political system to new political parties, not just two capitalist globalistic empire-building parties, not just one party that Red-baits and liberal-baits and the other that lives in fear of being

Red-baited and liberal-baited. We need to do what numerous other democracies have done and institute proportional representation, ready ballot access to dissident parties, convenient voter-registration conditions, public campaign funding for all candidates, and free TV time for all political parties.[1]

Real patriots are not afraid of dramatic changes—if they are in a democratic direction. They want the fundamental democratization of the political process and the economy of this country. As Mark Twain put it more than a century ago, his loyalty was not to his country's institutions and officeholders as such. His loyalty was to its basic principles of democracy, to the understanding that "all political power is inherent in the people, and all free governments are founded on their authority and instituted for their benefit; and that they have *at all times* an undeniable and indefeasible right to *alter their form of government* in such a manner as they may think expedient"[2] [italics in the original].

In sum, real patriots are not enamored of the trappings of superpatriotism but are interested in the substance of social justice. A twelve-year-old named Charlotte Aldebron reminds us that we ought to give less attention to patriotism's icons and more to its human content.

> The American flag stands for the fact that cloth can be very important. It is against the law to let the flag touch the ground or to leave the flag flying when the

weather is bad. The flag has to be treated with respect. You can tell just how important this cloth is because when you compare it to people, it gets much better treatment. Nobody cares if a homeless person touches the ground. A homeless person can lie all over the ground all night long without anyone picking him up, folding him neatly and sheltering him from the rain. School children have to pledge loyalty to this piece of cloth every morning. No one has to pledge loyalty to justice and equality and human decency. No one has to promise that people will get a fair wage, or enough food to eat, or affordable medicine, or clean water, or air free of harmful chemicals. But we all have to promise to love a rectangle of red, white, and blue cloth.[3]

☆

This concept of real patriotism is not a new notion. During the early part of the twentieth century, schoolteachers who were part of the Progressive movement advocated a "civic patriotism" in which the "work of a patriot is not so much to fight and die for his country, as it is to work and live to make it a grand nation."[4] In recent times we have seen stirrings all across the country. Consider the many real patriots who are not ready to trade in their civil liberties on the promise that an all-knowing, all-powerful government will keep them safe and sound.

Millions of Americans seem to agree that there is no safety in living under the abusive powers of a police state. In an Associate Press poll of September 2003, two-thirds of the respondents said they were concerned about the possible loss of freedom posed by laws supposedly designed to defend us from terrorism. By early 2004, more than 240 state and local governments across the United States had passed resolutions condemning the misnamed repressive Patriot Act, including the city of Chicago and the most populous county in America, Broward County of Florida, with 1.6 million people. The state governments of Hawaii, Alaska, and Vermont also renounced the act. And in November 2003 the House of Representatives voted to withdraw funds from two key provisions of the act.

Soon after, the American Civil Liberties Union reported a considerable increase in membership in 2003, and it was joined in its work against repressive legislation by several conservative groups and individuals, including the Eagle Forum. The American Bar Association formally denounced military tribunals and attorney-client monitoring. The American Library Association issued a protest against the section of the Patriot Act that allowed federal law officers to obtain records of our reading and computer usage at libraries, and prohibited librarians from warning us about it.[5]

Meanwhile, fewer Americans are equating militarism with patriotism. In 2003, the National Lawyers Guild reported that rising numbers of soldiers were seeking legal assistance in refusing to fight or attempting to withdraw from the armed services. And the number of young people who say they would never consider joining the military rose from 40 percent in 1980 to 64 percent in 2000, even though job opportunities diminished during that period. Nor did the 9/11 events boost recruitment or reverse the trend.[6] This does not mean that young people love their country less, just that they do not wish to devote themselves to the risks and horrors of war.

Almost two-thirds of Americans in one survey agreed with the statement: "The US plays the role of world policeman more than it should"; and only 12 percent thought that the US should continue as "preeminent world leader in solving international problems."[7] Once again the people are ahead of their leaders not because they are so much smarter but because they have their own genuine interests at heart rather than those of the global aggrandizers.

☆

Finally, real patriots are internationalists. They feel a special attachment to their own country but not in some competitive way that pits the United States against other powers. They regard the people of all nations as different members of the same human family.

In 1936, individuals from many countries and all walks of life joined together to form the International Brigade, which fought in Spain to protect democracy from the fascist forces of Generalissimo Franco. Charles Nusser, a veteran of that great struggle, relates this incident of international patriotism: "Sam Gonshak and I, both Spanish Civil War veterans, were in Guernica on June 1, 1985 [to commemorate the Spanish Civil War]. . . . I will never forget the speech of the organizer of the gathering. He referred to Sam and me as 'Patriots of the World.' Not patriots of the United States but 'Patriots of the World.' There have always been too many patriots in various countries straining to get at the throats of patriots in other countries."[8]

"Patriots of the World" who happen to live in the United States want to stop destroying others with jet bombers and missiles and US-financed death squads and start healing this nation. This is not just a good and noble ideal, it is a historical necessity. It is the best kind of security. Sooner or later Americans rediscover that they cannot live on flag-waving alone. They begin to drift off into reality, confronted by the economic irrationalities and injustices of a system that provides them with the endless circuses and extravaganzas of superpatriotism, heavy tax burdens, a crushing national debt and military budget, repeated bloodletting in foreign lands, and sad neglect of domestic needs, denying them the bread of prosperity and their birthright as democratic citizens. We need a return to reality. We need to unveil the lies and subterfuges that so advantage the wealthy plutocracy. We need to pursue policies at home and abroad that serve the real needs of humanity. Then we can love our country—and peace and justice too.

1. For instance, see the electoral reforms initiated by the Sandinista government in Nicaragua, in Michael Parenti, "Is Nicaragua More Democratic Than the United States?" *CovertAction Information Bulletin*, summer 1986, 48–50, 52.

2. Maxwell Geismar, ed., *Mark Twain and the Three R's* (New York: Bobbs-Merrill, 1973), 179–80; the quotation is from Twain's novel, *A Connecticut Yankee in King Arthur's Court* (1889).

3. Charlotte Aldebron, "What the American Flag Stands For," *Heartland Review Quarterly*, October 2002.

4. Quoted in O'Leary, *To Die For*, 192.

5. Jennifer Van Bergen, "Bush, Media, and the Bill of Rights," 9 July 2003, http://www.truthout.org.

6. *San Francisco Chronicle*, 2 March 2003; and Van Bergen, "Bush, Media and the Bill of Rights."

7. Survey reported by Foreign Policy in *Focus*, 1 May 2003, www.fpif.org.

8. Charles Nusser, letter to the *Nation*, 6–13 January 1992 (italics in the original).

Printed in the USA
CPSIA information can be obtained
at www.ICGtesting.com
JSHW082341140824
68134JS00020B/1817

9 780872 864337